RESISTANCE

THE CLANDESTINE
RADIO OPERATORS

Jean-Louis PERQUIN

SOE, BCRA, OSS

Histoire&
Collections

CONTENTS

Previous page.
**Type 3 Mk II radio set pictured with a 9X19 mm UD M 42 SMG,
two Mills hand grenades and a battery being reloaded...**

Right.
**Re-enactement picture depicting a clandestine radio operator
with a Polish A1 Nelka radio set.**
*(O. Blanc-Brude picture, radio set belonging to P. Giraud of the Amicale
des transmissions de la Côte d'Azur)*

Above.
Radio operators
in the Vercors area
in 1944 in La Britière:
left to right, standing:
Mercier, Cendral, Bennes,
Montefusco, Garnot;
kneeling: Lacourt-Winant
and Lassalle.
(Robert Bennes picture,
Musée des Troupes de
Montagne collection)

THE CLANDESTINE RADIO OPERATORS

IT IS IMPORTANT to pay tribute to those who lost their lives for Freedom during what can now be described as a genuine war fought on the electromagnetic spectrum between 1940 and 1944: radio operators, liaison and close protection agents, clerks and the numerous volunteers who housed them, who provided shelter for the emissions, hid the equipment and carried out many other services and without whom nothing would have been possible and to whom we owe so much.

The aim of this book is to show some of the clandestine radio equipment used by the agents infiltrated in occupied France in order to establish contact with London and then Alger (from the end of 1942). As the technical radio part is so complex and aimed at specialists, it is necessary to point out that this study has no other objective than to give a presentation of the different radios equipments used during the period; one should keep in mind that many different models existed with several variations because of the constant technical evolution which was all the more important during the war. It is also interesting to note that certain short wave radios were specially adapted for naval use (like the S-Phone for clandestine maritime operations) while others, initially meant for naval operations, were adapted for clandestine receptions (like the U.S. Navy RBZ receiver for example).

Moreover, some changes were made in the field, as some officers found the suitcases too distinctive and preferred to exchange them for French models or even hide the B2 transceiver in a household radio receiver!!

Tribute needs to be paid to Pierre Lorain who presented the majority of these clandestine equipments in his work: "Armement clandestin France 1941-1944" published by Plon in 1974 and then is a series of articles "SOE le cheval de Troie de sa Majesté" in the French Gazette des Armes monthly (n° 17, 18 and 33 in June and July 1974 and then in the December 1975 magazine).

Above.
Radio operator in action.
(Georges Ricard)

Below.
1942 Vintage SSTR1 American radio set.
(Jean-Louis Perquin)

Right.
An iconic image of the struggle over the electromagnetic spectrum, a radio operator emits with a Type B Mk II suitcase radio while a close protection agent overwatches the street.
(Josiane Somers)

THE PIANISTS:
THE MEN AND WOMEN OF FREEDOM

Right at the heart of a merciless struggle against the German forces, the radio operators only had a six month life expectancy. They knew of these all too often fatal odds longs before they were infiltrated by parachute, boat or airplane on a clandestine airstrip. These agents were true crusaders, if not the real Kamikaze, of Free France.

These highly specialized shadow fighters – men and women - were capable of emitting radio traffic at high speed without error or distinctive sign, of coding without fault, and of selecting and changing emitting locations frequently and with discretion despite the omnipresent enemy. No mean achievement even when one is twenty year of age and has courage to spare. Having an unfaltering courage was necessary to accept being the prey in a merciless and relentless hunt. In the final confrontation, surrounded by the enemy, some have not hesitated to commit suicide or to fight to the end in a hopeless battle to finally die at the hands of the enemy; others were captured, tortured and disappeared forever. For the BCRA (*Bureau Central de Renseignements et d'Action* or Central Bureau for Intelligence and Operations), the Free French intelligence service, the assessment was not even open for discussion and the figures were frightening : 8 out of 11 agents killed

in 1941, 12 out of 15 in 1942 and 15 out of 19 in 1943. The percentage of deaths therefore rose to 75% between 1941 and 1942 and up to 50 % during the first 6 months of 1943. It then dropped to 25% thanks to the adoption of the Electre plan.

Each radio emission requires a long and dangerous preparation phase performed by the liaison agent and the close protection agent; to protect the radio operator, they would expose themselves in his place because they knew that without communications, the entire mission would have be encarried out in vain. They carried the equipment and weapons from the caches where they were stored to the point of emission. They carried the particularly incriminating coded messages. Weapons in hand, they secured the outskirts of the emission area and they protected the radio operator while he sent his messages. They were constantly on the move, by vehicle and by train. They faced controls and searches from all the police forces, both German and also, unfortunately, French. They constantly had to prove their courage, composure and ingenuity to get out of unforeseeable and critical situations. These particularly difficult conditions did not stop the number of broadcasts to be multiplied by one hundred between 1943 and 1944!

Above.
A covert radio operator in action. Notice the simultaneous use of two suitcase radios!
(Georges Ricard collection)

Opposite page.
A covert radio operator in action with the Maquis with a very close protection team.
(Josiane Somers collection)

Above.
In the city of Lyon, in 1944, Paul Brun and Paul Favre were pictured while emitting covertly with a Mk XV set.
(Georges Ricard)

Below.
The Vineyards, "STS 35", in Beaulieu. This is where, from the Spring of 1942, the special individual security course for W/T radio operators was taught.
(Josianne Somers)

The Electre plan

This plan which was the work of both Jean Fleury[1] (Colonel Panier, Grec, Latin 1) and Jean Roy (Commandant Valois) was activated in July 1943. The separation of transmission and reception was one of its most important innovations thereby reducing considerably the exposure to German Goniometers (DF). Night emissions were stopped as they were too noticeable because of their long wave lengths. Each radio operator received a new transmission plan reproduced on a microfilm, called «purple plan» for odd days and «black plan» for even ones. Each plan consists of ten frequencies (thus ten quartz). Radiomen would only move with the quartz that were smaller and more easily hidden than a radio. The heavy radios of the beginning of the war were by then obsolescent and they were replaced by less awkward and better quality sets. The duration of the emissions had to be less than 30 minutes. In only a few months, 2,000 transceivers were produced and more than 1,000 quartz were cut, a considerable achievement for the UK industry in a war period.

After the implementation of this plan, the losses dropped to 25% while traffic considerably increased from 120-149 per day from France to England and 80-100 in the opposite direction to 50,000 for 1944 alone.

---

1. Jean Fleury infiltrated in France by Pickup during the night of 26 to 27 January 1943 on the « Courgette » field near Lons le Saunier and exfiltrated, also by Pickup, during the night of 13 to 14 February 1943.

Right.
A Type A Mk II suitcase radio.
(Jean-Paul Lescure)

Below.
A page of radio codes.
(Jean-Paul Lescure)

Below.
A rather impressive bench used to store quartz in the STS 53A "Home Station" in Grendon, the control radio station of the SOE in the United Kingdom.
(Bruno Barthelot collection)

01

```
 1  SXKDJ  NIUFM  VMURK  SZTJQ  YWKME
 2  YOKIZ  QVAUR  PZNBP  IPCCH  SQFNW
 3  ZHCWD  YLMLN  ASQZG  GYQJB  CAHZS
 4  PYGPM  BEJYX  UWBUR  DIQFS  JHQWJ
 5  NVNYP  RFXUP  TQWAD  RFOPH  ESCCS
 6  UTEZN  PBGUM  SVRMJ  ZKWYA  CSFHK
 7  IXXPO  NNJSS  DLHEZ  BZBFM  KOAMW
 8  TPPGD  SXOMN  KNVRW  ZPZKX  IRBOA
 9  ZJOPA  NPDGU  RHXZY  SRTZO  VIMCO
10  RPMST  HZOJY  GSFVU  VKNIT  VIDAN
11  VFZBB  SVIYM  UQSPJ  DHWNF  GKJEO
12  NPHLH  FJOGI  TVPSF  QXKSE  WKUAI
13  MASOW  HEEDZ  JKZVR  HNYTI  QFRNP
14  ISYTP  BDLCY  IRFCW  BXNFL  UCMYH
15  QPNHV  FCOUB  CEAUF  LYWKR  EFNZO
16  ZKCJC  ZVVJF  OKPMD  WGDTS  VFOOU
17  AVNVY  MABGD  YWICV  LQPRG  WOTHO
18  AEVUQ  QHDSB  GWAOC  RXFDZ  CBPTY
19  AEPKA  CSDOR  LRMVX  ISGLY  JHZCL
20  TFHHD  VZNFG  DSTRY  KEUBX  CLAWL
21  LAOUC  TRIEH  XRHVZ  QBMQP  JKLKS
22  ZYDNB  TWPKO  XIQHW  YKZHK  DJMMG
23  ARQDZ  UOZFP  YSSHV  RJCAM  NZGJB
24  UFKHL  QIRYC  VKGSX  WQWDG  EUANK
25  IZJRE  TKUWJ  BYUIK  LAWVF  EXPIN
```

THE TRAINING

In June 1941, BCRA Captain R. Lagier selected 21 FFL (Free French) paratroopers in order to use them for clandestine operations. They were based in Inchmery, which became a training centre for French agents and adopted the code name of « Station 36 ».

On 15 August 1941, some new French trainees arrived. This batch was composed of three officers, including Aspirant (officer cadet) Louis Kerjean and 10 men, including Georges Brault, Georges Ledoux and Daniel Cordier. They were supervised by Paul Schmidt who later was to be parachuted into France. It is also during this month of August 1941 that General de Gaulle visited them for the first time. Training was then carried out over a 6 months period.

The British had several schools. Initially, the radio operators were trained by the Royal Corps of Signal at STS 52. (Special Training School No 52), located at Thame Park, Oxfordshire. *"This is one of these many 'country houses' - in France we say: castle. This is where the candidates for the great adventure learn clandestine radio, and two or three other small things. Learning Morse of course, but also the art of the gun taught by a former Hong Kong police chief. ...One learns how to bury a parachute without leaving too many traces, how to encode telegrams, how to hide a message in a seemingly insignificant text, to use invisible inks… And one is taught how to drive an automobile.*

And what if we get caught? It will be an unpleasant experience. One tablet of cyanide to swallow to escape from it all, that is part of the toolbox. But there is no obligation to use it. It's your choice. No one can say in advance what he will do under torture: try not to talk, talk as little as possible, as late as possible, take at least three days so that the news of your arrest has time to be known by your friends, and so improve their chances of survival. It depends on the resilience of your body and your mind, and the skill of your torturer... All things that we can discover only for ourselves... For the Catholics, to whom the Church forbids suicide, a priest wrote a document explaining how to swallow his cyanide pill with a peaceful conscience."

As specific as they were, these "schools" were cast in the same mould and met the same standards. They were located in large comfortable countryside houses. Hidden in the back of gardens, they attempted to be as discreet as possible. Around twenty trainees could be accommodated in those houses under excellent conditions. A team of «batmen», skilfull and devoted, entirely composed of British soldiers, was in charge of maintenance, cooking and daily chores. These servicemen tidied the rooms,

Right.
Milton Hall, Jedburgs take a class on Morse code
(National Archives)

10

Above.
Milton Hall, Jedburghs
during a signal class.
(National Archives)

served meals at the table and did the laundry. In this way, the trainees who were free from any "admin" tasks could devote themselves entirely to the theoretical and practical classes that were given them. Under the control of a Major, a team of hand-picked subject matters experts, both officers and NCOs, taught those classes with a typically British mix of skills, conscience and thoroughness. Every morning, the Major inspected his staff, man-by-man and button-by-button. He supervised the exercises closely as well as the state of mind of his trainees. Security remained one of his prime concern. Just like surprise, secret was, according to him, one of the pre-condition for success on the battlefield.

At the end of these courses, the trainees carried out practical exercises including clandestine radio emis-

sions from surrounding towns. A special school (STS) for non-British radio operators was located in Hans Place, London, a very short distance from Brompton Road. In that school, the use of Morse code, the drafting of messages and radio techniques were taught. An STS dedicated to Signals skills was also created in Bedford.

In Autumn 1941, following the numerous loss suffered by those specialists and considering how such losses were threatening the very existence of the networks, the SOE decided to create a security course in Gendon, Buckinghamshire. This was later transferred to Beaulieu, STS 35 "Vineyards", in the Spring of 1942. The radio trainees were separated from other agents, as they were too vulnerable in the field.

- STS 40 t in "Howbury House", Waterend, Bedfordshire, was opened in September 1943 for the training on the new beacons used for clandestine air operations (S-Phone and Eureka/Rebecca portable ground-based beacons). The class lasted for 10 days. This school was also used by the Jedburghs in January 1944.
- STS 53a - Grendon Hall, near Aylesbury, Buckinghamshire, encryption school.
- STS 53b - Poundon House, Buckinghamshire, for radio emission and reception.
- STS 54 - radio operators school (used by the Jedburghs in December 1943).
- STS 54a - Fawley Court, Henley on Thames.
- STS 54b - Belhaven School, Dunbar.

Right.
Milton Hall, a French Jedburgh Captain takes note of a message.
(National Archives)

Below.
Inchmery house, also known as STS 36, was the first training establishment for the French agents.
(Roger Flamand collection)

...EMBER THE ENEMY IS LISTENING

Above.
**At the other end
of the chain, an inside
view of the "Home Station"
in England, STS 53A,
located in Grendon.**
(IWM)

- STS 51. Jump school in Ringway near Manchester, two, then three houses isolated but close to the base served as accommodations for the SOE trainees:
- STS 51a, Dunham House, Charcoal Lane, Dunham Massy, Altrincham, Cheshire.
- STS 51b, Fulshaw Hall, Alderley Road, Wilmslow, Cheshire.

- STS 51c, York House, Timperley, Cheshire.

The school provided a five-day training course; 75 SOE agents followed it. In Ringway, under SOE sponsorship, 872 SIS trainees followed the parachute course including the Sussex mission as well as 172 SAS Troopers.

Several memos issued by BCRA in 1943 allow for a better comprehension of the radio operator training:

Left.
**An aerial view of Beaulieu, "The finishing school"
where STS 35, the school for covert agents,
was located.**
(DR)

Opposite page, top.
**The Jedburgh school in Milton Hall: a Morse code
lesson. Stewart Alsop can be identified on the right.**

Opposite page.
**An aerial view of "Military establishment 65" (ME65)
based in Milton Hall, less than a dozen kilometers
away from Peterborough, Northamptonshire.**
(Bertrand Souquet collection)

Patriotic School (security investigation on the agent): 2 weeks.

Camberley (issue of kit and identity pictures): 1 week.
- STS 51 (parachute training in Ringway): 1 week.
- STS 6 (West Court: paramilitary training, weapons handling and sabotage): 2 week.
- STS 52 (Thames Park radio school): from 3 to 4 months.

In May 1943, the BCRA issued a memo revealing how training was conducted at STS 52. It was divided into 2 phases:

General training

- Security lecture (common to all agents).
- Tailing, counter-tailing, identification, security measures in trains, stations, etc… dead letter boxes, individual protection.

- Parachuting exercises.
- Exercises with Lysander airplane.

Training on signals, radio electrical transmissions and radio techniques

- Radio theory: electricity and radio electricity.
- Radio practice: operating and maintaining a radio set.
- Radio broadcasting: Morse code (4 to 6 weeks), procedures (3 weeks), codes.
- Practical Field Exercise: the radio operator had to set up his emission base in a British provincial town. The operator had to extend his wire antenna, then send some messages and finally receive some messages. He had to operate safely and discreetly, contact Home Station, take "scheds" (radio schedules) and QRX and be capable of taking the initiative when needed. These exercises could last up to a week and depending on the results, the student operator could be ordered to repeat it.

> *I think it is the right moment to convey the congratulations of our higher command for the superb achievements of those who have dedicated their strength, and in several occasions, their lives, in order to continuously provide the Allied forces with a constant flow of intelligence; despite the very high risks they were running, they kept on operating until those groups of agents were, on several occasions, overrun by the enemy. I was informed that, in May 1944 alone, and even though each broadcast was in itself dangerous for the radio operator, those organisations sent, by ways of clandestine radio emissions, 700 situation reports.*
>
> **General Bedell Smith, Chief of Staff of General Eisenhower**

Left.
Ringway Parachute training School (STS 51). Adjusting the standard issue British Type X parachute. Parachute students boarding an aircraft in Ringway under the watchful eyes of an RAF "Dispatcher".
(Aldershot Parachute School Museum)

Below.
Ringway, STS 51, a parachute drop from a Whitley V.

A memo issued by the BCRA dated 19th July, 1943 on the new training organization specified that radio training classes should be as follows:
- Ability to send and receive Morse code divided into 5 groups (from beginner to 14 words per minute, WPM).
- Emission of both letters & numerals.
- Listening to Morse on a commercial radio.
- Special Q Code.
- Special service operating rules.
- Operating as a Network (classroom work).
- Electricity and Wireless Transmission (8 hours).

In 1943, the British established a SOE training centre - code name: Massingham – at the Club des Pins, West of Algiers. The Americans of the OSS chose to set up shop downtown, at the villa Magnol. Most of the agents who were to be sent to France received all or part of their specialised trainings in these two locations.

Ringway Parachute training School (STS 51).
A balloon jump with a Type X parachute.
Notice the camouflaged canopy.

Top left.
Balloon jump in Ringway. A trainee makes a perfect jump standing at attention!
(Aldershot Parachute School Museum)

Above.
Team Ivor. Left to right: American radio operator First Sergeant Lewis Goddard "Oregon", British Captain John Howard Cox "Monmouth" and Lieutenant Robert Colin "Selune". This team was parachuted during the night of August 6 to 7 near Beddes 6 km from Chateaumeillant in the Indre département. It landed outside the intended DZ and this led to very severe consequences: Coxtombe fell in a hole and sprained his ankle, Colin also fell in another hole, accidentaly shot himself through the leg with his own pistol while Goddard's jump ended tragically with his accidental death. Note the use of the Oversmock over the camouflaged Denison Smock.

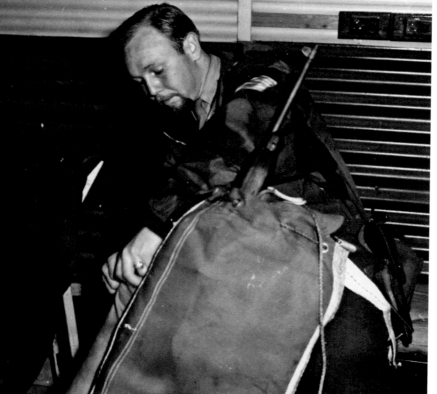

Left.
Jedburgh Team Ivor. American radio operator, 1SGT Goddard, buckles up his Leg Bag from which the barrel of his USM1 A1 Carbine sticks up. Notice the Denison Smock with an american flag on the left shoulder as well as the .45 ACP M1911A1 pistol worn in a cross draw US 1916 holster.

Above.
The Aubrey Jedburgh Team. This Jedburgh team is one of the few to have jumped wearing civilian clothes because its area of operation was the North and East of Paris. They jumped on August 12 at 01:55 during Operation "Xavier" (Spiritulalist 6D for the RAF) near St Pathus Plessis-Belleville (in the Seine et Marne département). From left to right: French Lieutenant A. Chaigneau "Koldare" alias J. Telmon who was killed on 08/27/1944 near Oissery; center is British Captain Godfrey Marchant "Rutland", team leader; seated is British radio NCO Ivor Alfred Hooker "Thaler".

Right.
On August 4, 1944, on USAAF base Harrington, the Ronald Jedburgh team is getting ready to board its transport aircraft. This team was composed of French Lieutenant George Deseilligny (J. Dartigues) "Bouton", of American First Lieutenant Shirly Ray Trumps "Boursier" and of Sergeant Elmer B. Esch, the radio, alias "Pound". A fourth paratrooper was added to this mission, a French radio, Second Lieutenant Paul Dumas, "Piémontais". They jumped on August 5th at 0309 in the Vannes (Brittany) region. Trumps faces the camera and behind him Esch, Deseilligny (with a sidecap) and Dumas (back) can be identified. If Trumps wears a markedly American combat outfit composed of a reinforced paratrooper jacket and an OSS Stiletto attached to the holster of his Colt .45 M1911A1 pistol. *(National Archives)*

THE FIRST MISSIONS

GEORGES BEGUÉ, who parachuted on the night of 5th to 6th May 1941 over Vatan near Valençay (17 km north of Châteauroux), was the first SOE radio operator. He worked for the "Ventriloquist" network of SOE F and used his own first name as a code name, which then became the first radios usual code name: Georges 2, 3, 4, etc. From 1942 on, SOE F (a British service) used first names found on calendars while the BCRA (SOE RF) used French or English names such as Cadoux, Gazelle, Bass, Fabulous and associated the letter code W [1] to their chief's code (Tab-W,

---

1. W "Wireless" radio transmission

Above.
Badge of the Special Forces Club depicting a clandestine agent being dropped over occupied territories.
(Etienne Preney)

Left.
A mannequin wearing a jump suit worn during the "Dentelle" Sussex mission which was parachuted near Alençon on July 7, 1944. It is holding the top part of a back protective cushion.
(Dominique Soulier, Sussex Museum)

Right.
Jedburgh Team Aubrey which was dropped during "Operation Spiritualist 6" from "Fightin 'Sam", a B-24 D serial number 42-40506 R commanded by an American pilot named Moser. This particular picture is interesting because it depicts a typical mix of attires: an SOE helmet, a Denison Smock and a civilian suit ... Note the low quarter shoes and the shoelaces used as trousers ties for bicycle riding as well as the strange looking parcel. Notice the British regulation canteen and the barrel of a US M1 Carbine sticking out of the bundle. The team was dropped on August 12 around 0155 at Le Plessis-Belleville. Left to right: French Lieutenant A. Chaigneau "Koldare" British Captain Godfrey Marchand "Rutland" and, standing, British radio operator Ivor Alfred Hooker, carelessly holding a cigarette over the parachute of the bundle in spite of security regulations prohibiting the use of cigarettes around parachute canopies.
(National Archives)

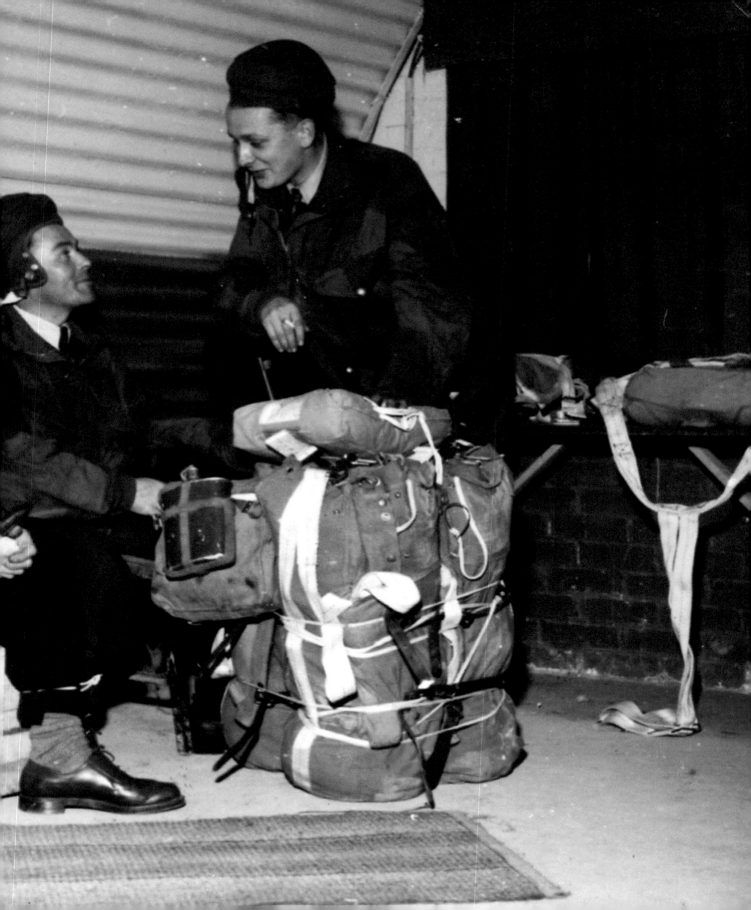

SIF-W…). From the second semester of 1943, other words reflecting the names of the inhabitants of either a nation, a region, a town or even an ethnic group were used such as Afghan, Brésilien, Béarnais, Troyen or Maure, for example.

Between July and October 1941, six French agents were infiltrated in France making up three teams each composed of a commander and a radio operator. Out of the 28 radio operators trained in Inchmery House and parachuted between 1941 and 1942, 26 were captured: 1 was incarcerated, 9 were executed and 16 were deported.

Right.
SOE Agent doing a training jump.
(Roger Flamand)

Right.
Mannequin wearing a jump suit. Notice how gas protection overboots are worn since they were considered as more watertight than SOE overboots.
(Charlie Roussel, private collection)

Top right.
Georges Bégué in London. Parachuted "Blind" during the night of the 5 to the 6 of May 1941 in the Vatan region close to Valençay (17 km North of Chateauroux), he operated in support of the "Ventriloquist" network of SOE F.
(Josiane Somers collection)

Previous page, right.
Ringway, STS 51, a parachute trainee, his canopy fully deployed, legs together and knees ready to absorb the shock pictured only seconds before hitting the ground.

Previous page, left.
Going through "the hole" in an Albermale bomber.
(IWM)

Previous page, bottom right.
Type A Mk II radio set.
(Jean-Paul Lescure)

> " *The radio service, that Julitte had started organizing in situ, was also operating under the supervision of the delegate who was, each month, visiting London and receiving hundreds, and latter thousands of telegrams, forever moving its radio sets once located by the enemy direction finding equipment while at the same time compensating the heavy losses it suffered.* "
>
> **Général De Gaulle** *Mémoires de Guerre*

TALES OF RADIO OPERATORS

THE FIRST STORY PERTAINS to the network of LIEUTENANT-COLONEL George Reginald Starr, DSO, MC, (Hilaire, Gaston) Its area of operation was the R4 zone from Vierzon to the Pyrenees.

On the 8th of November 1942, Lieutenant Marcus Bloom (Urbain) (Prunus network) made a covert landing from a felucca crewed by Polish sailors near Cassis on the French Riviera. On the 12th of April 1943, in Toulouse, Bloom and another dozen people belonging to the network were arrested by the Germans.

During the night of the 22nd to 23rd of August 1943, Starr welcomed his first radio operator by parachute, a woman named Yvonne Cormeau (Annette, Fairy). Thanks to her work nearly

Above, opposite page bottom right.
For the "Now it can be told" film which was shot in 1944, Jacqueline Nearne re-enacted her role as agent "Cat". Jacqueline followed was trained at the STS before being parachuted under the alias of "Josette Norville". She operated as a liaison officer for the "Stationer" SOE F network. *(Document* Now it can be told*)*

Next page, top.
An obviously posed picture taken towards the end of the war showing a radio operator with a close protection team... *(Georges Ricard)*

Left.
Yvonne Cormeau, AKA "Annette" and "Fairy" was a wireless radio operator for the "Wheelwright" SOE F network. She was parachuted during the night of the 22nd to the 23rd of August 1943 in the Bordeaux region. *(Josiane Somers collection)*

Type A Mk III radio Set.
(Jean-Paul Lescure)

147 parachute drops were carried in support of the network. Yvonne worked tirelessly until the Liberation, transmitting some 400 radio messages, which considering the circumstances, was a remarkable achievement.

To provide her protection, almost 200 houses were made available for her emissions. During the first few months, she changed position every week leaving an average distance of 100 km between each emission point. Then, for the next 4 months, she only had to move once a month. These safe houses were always situated in isolated and remote locations; their owners could thus observe any suspicious movement and immediately alert their clandestine guests if anything seemed untoward. Even if the Germans were really persistent in their efforts at finding the clandestine transmitter, there was no serious danger for the operator of being "DF'd" by the enemy as Starr had organised a 150 km wide security zone around the emission points. This "screen" would invariably detect any suspicious vehicular activity. Towards the end of the war, the main problem was the interference of the radio broadcasts carried out by the Germans.

On the 11th of April 1944 Lieutenant Denis Parsons (Pierrot) was parachuted as a second radio operator for

Above.
MK7 Paraset radio set used in a French Maquis.
(Georges Ricard)

Opposite page, top.
Jacqueline Nearne, agent "Cat", takes note of a message she has received with her Type 3 Mk II radio set.

Opposite page, bottom right.
Jacqueline Nearne, agent "Cat", operates her Type 3 Mk II radio set.
(Now it can be told documents)

Colonel Starr. He was an efficient member of the team and by transmitting 84 messages he also contributed to the success of many resupply drops. He joined the Maquis after the D-day and was injured during the fighting in Castelnau on 21st June 1944.

SOE F STATIONER network

This network was under the command of Squadron Leader Maurice Southgate, (Hector, Maurice, Philippe). On the 25th of January 1943, Southgate was parachuted for his first mission with Jacqueline Nearne[2], his messenger. He had to contact Mr. Octave Chantraine,

2. Jacqueline Nearne can be seen on several pictures because she played the role of a parachuted agent in the movie *"Now it can be told"* shot in 1947. As it was shot immediately after the war this movie is a real reference showing a large range of the SOE material; it is available in DVD at the Imperial War Museum.

Testament letter of Pierrette Louin

Below.
This bronze sculpture located in the Mont Valérien near Paris based on a work by Claude Grange is an allegory of the Free French Air Force (FAFL): "Despite the talons of the vultures that are inexorably closing, communications go through and missions are fulfilled" ("Liaisons by Pickup and air drops", this work also represents the image of a clandestine radio operator).
(J.-L. Perquin)

Pierrette Louin, a radio operator parachuted during the night of 5th to 6th April in the Limoges area, was arrested by the Gestapo on the 27th April 1944, deported and hung in Ravensbrück on the 18th January 1945. Declared "having died for France", Pierrette Louin was mentioned in the army corps dispatches and awarded the Croix de Guerre with Palm and the Resistance Medal.

«Dear all.

Before leaving for the big adventure, I wanted to tell you everything myself. It may be of some consolation to you as I am no longer alive if you are reading this. I know this may cause you grief but if there is one thing, which will perhaps not lessen the pain, but make it less bitter, is that my death will not have been in vain, it served France.

You must not be too sad as this is the only kind of death I could have hoped for, because it is the most beautiful. My age does not count, the important thing is that I am not going to the fight as if I was part of an anonymous herd only fighting because "that's the way it is", because one has to do it.

I am a volunteer-and this means a lot- it is something stronger than a simple word- it chiefly means a conscious

choice. *This mission that I will maybe never return from, I have not suffered it like an order; I have neither accepted it not knowing what I was letting myself in for. No. I thought about it and I made my choice. My soul agreed to it and from that moment giving my life no longer was a sacrifice. Still, I cherish life. I can feel within me a strength and a taste for the fight which could win my whole life over. But I could not keep that strength, nor have a desire for life if I was to shy away from what my spirit feels. And what I feel is no longer the sentimental jingoism of my youth. It is something which is part of me, it is the love for France. A passion, which is now an instinct, but a clear-sighted passion, devoid of any ridiculous sentimentality. I am not going to fight for words, ideas or people. I am not going to fight either against words, ideas or other people but I am going to fight to save an ensemble which just cannot disappear, a type of life, an ideal, France. I cannot explain this but I can feel France in me and this the reason why I have chosen to leave, why I did not want to be the impotent passer-by who thinks suffering with words is enough, why I refused to exchange my life for my soul. For all this, I have joined the forces. Then luck quickly came to me.*

In July I was one of the two girls who were offered the opportunity of active service. In a second I had accepted. I thus joined Military Intelligence. In September, I arrived in London by plane. My technical training was followed by a course to become a clandestine radio operator. I then followed the parachute course. After a first failed attempt in November, there has been days of waiting and fever and then again hope : I will jump in a few days.

Thus, on a soon to come moonless night, an airplane will take me over France. I will do a parachute jump and I will carry out my mission. I will have forged ID papers and covert radio equipment. My mission will be to send by radio messages to London and Algiers all the intelligence the agents and I will gather. I am well aware of all the dangers that surround me. I know I stand little chances of returning alive. The least I risk is to be jailed in a fortress somewhere in Germany. But does it really matters since I will have put up a fight ? If I die, these are the rules of the game, no regrets, no bitterness since my soul will be untouched. If I am to live, I will have earnt the right to live and the joy of having remained faithful to my ideal.

But I think of you, who will remain behind, and it causes me much grief. But I know you will understand and approve of me. We will be reunited. I bid you farewell, without any sadness. Once again, I kiss you with all my heart. Pierrette"

(AASSDN document)

president of the Fédération Paysanne (Peasant Federation) of the Indre department, as well as Captain C.T. Rechenman (Julian) and to develop the Tinker network which had been created by Major Cowburn (Benoît) in the Châteauroux-Tarbes area.

On 14th April 1943, Major René A. Louis Maingard (Samuel) was parachuted into France in order to assist Southgate as a radio operator. Soon, the supply drops started.

On 2nd September 1943 at 0830, the Gestapo forced its way into the Neraud family home in Clermont-Ferrand and arrested the whole family: father, mother and daughter. Their home was used as a safe house and the main meeting point for the Stationer network. Their name had been given to many agents when leaving England as a first contact in France. During the search, the Gestapo agents

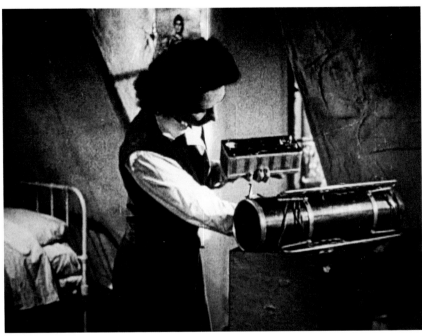

Above and right.
"Cat", AKA Jacqueline Nearne, uncovers a Type A Mk II radio set hidden in a vacuum cleaner.
(*Now it can be told document*)

found a suitcase containing 200,000 Francs as well as gold coins. Collette Neraud and her mother were deported to Ravensbrück and her father to Buchenwald where he died on 23 March 1945. Her mother died on 31st January 1945 in Ravensbrück. Only Collette, the daughter, survived. She was repatriated by Sweden in 1945.

Major Maingard trained a local radio operator, Pierre Hirsh (Popaul), who, after two months of training, was confirmed as operational by London. He transmitted from Montluçon.

Jacqueline Nearne was the sister of Eileen Mary Nearne (Rose) (Bricklayer network).

Above and left.
An SOE packing line. Workers wrap suitcase radios in Wire-type canvas and metal wire baskets before a para drop.
(Now it can be told *documents*)

Above.
Wire-type airdrop metal basket and its parachute having been used in operation to drop a radio set (red marking and triangle).
(Mathan collection and picture)

Left.
Wire-type airdrop metal basket and its parachute. Notice the easy to spot parachute and the red marking complete with triangle indicating a radio set.
(Musée de la Résistance et de la Déportation de Nantua collection)

Right.
René Bouvret alias "Chinois" was betrayed while he was operating his radio set on 4 January 1944 in Hauteville in the Ain département. Surrounded by the Gestapo, he chose to shoot himself in the head rather than be caught alive. He was made a Compagnon de la Libération.
(Musée de l'ordre de la Libération collection)

Right.
Two Jedburgh teams radio operators: Frenchman Jean Sassi and his friend British Sergeant Ronald Eric Chatten posing for the photographer. Left is French sous-lieutenant (2LT) Jean Sassi "Latimer" a member of the "Chloroform" Team who was dropped at 0015, on 30 June 1944 on DZ "Framboise" in Dieulefit close to Comps by a B-24 belonging to 885 Bomb Squadron, 15th Air Force. This plane had taken off the day before at 2035 from Blida, French Algeria. The team was under the command of French Captain Jacques Martin "Lionel" with American lieutenant Henry Mac Intosh "Joshua" as deputy. Jean Sassi carried out another mission codenamed "Vega". Led by Captain Hérenguel "Dewavrant" and lieutenant Pénin "Puget", this French team jumped into Northern Laos in Nam Vat (Muong Ngam) on 04 June1945. Right: British Sergeant Ronald Eric Chatten "Artus", radio operator of Team "Chrysler". This team was composed of British Captain Cyril Herbert Sell "Elie" and French Captain Paul Aussaresses "Bazin". The team was dropped on the 16th of August 1944 at 2330 on DZ "Fliberty" in the Ariège département. Notice that Chatten wears his SF badge on the left chest rather than on the right shoulder. According to SOE tradition, this indicated he had already carried out an operational mission.
(Jean Sassi collection)

Radios trained in occupied France

It is also important to emphasize the critical role played by radio operators who were trained inside occupied France. On the 265 radio operators that have so far been identified, at least 91 were trained in France. Locally recruited by radio operators who had received their training prior to the beginning of the war, or even by radio hams, they were introduced to specific covert techniques and then tested by the British before being finally certified. If the training was sometimes conducted by a radio operator who was dropped in support of a network, other operators were trained in real "schools". For example, 53 radio operators were trained by the BCRA in one of these training centers located in a series of farms near Chambarran, North-West of Grenoble.

Left.
Type A Mk II radio set emitting.
(Georges Ricard)

After parachuting into France, she first went to Clermont-Ferrand then to Châteauroux. Her work involved a lot of travelling from Tarbes to Poitiers, Toulouse, Paris and Pau. She often bluffed her way trough the German controls by using her chemical laboratory representative status. She received an M.B.E. and the "Croix de Guerre" and was introduced to Her Majesty The Queen.

A radio operator among others: René Bouvrand, alias "Martial", "Opel", "Chinois"

Originally from Arc-les-Gray in the Haute-Saône department, René Bouvrand joined the Air Force school in Rochefort, and graduated as a radio operator. The invasion of the free zone led him to leave the forces. In January 1943, he joined the "Résistance". Appointed to the Signals group under the authority of Jean Moulin, he became Martial. Very quickly his experience proved essential, and he broadcasted from several locations such as Louhans, Ambérieu and Montélimar. In June 1943, the transmissions were placed under the authority of André Montaut "MEC W"[3] Chrysler, and then under the authority of Nippon, a radio operator from London.

René was aware of the risks he took but his work ethos prevailed. He always carried a weapon during each broadcast, telling his friends that he would never be caught alive. On the 4th of January, during a broadcast in the region of Hauteville in the Ain district, René was caught by the detection services (DF) and the Gestapo despite being previously warned that he had been spotted.

He just had time to warn London and to destroy his radio transmitter. Then he fired at the Germans, shooting three before being shot himself. The same day, in the same area, radio operators Albert Meckies "Basque" and Fernand "Slovène" a radio operator recruited in France at the beginning of 1943, were arrested… Fernand was then posted as missing; René Bouvrand was posthumously made a Compagnion of the Ordre de la Libération.

Above.
In the film, "Félix", the head of the network, receives a second wireless operator who uses a B2 suitcase radio.
(Now it can be told document)

3. Mec W had been parachuted in occupied France with his mission leader, Captain Georges Weil, on 28th May 1942. Eighteen hours after his parachute insertion, Georges Weill was arrested by the Germans. He immediately committed suicide by swallowing a pill. His mission leader arrested, without any other contact, Mec W went back to England by crossing into Spain. There, he received a new mission. During this second mission, Mec W was arrested on 21st July 1943, and killed.

The tasks of the clandestine radio operators

CHEVEIGNE

Maurice Cheveigné AKA Eel was parachuted "blind" on 31 May 1942 at 2:00 AM. His first mission was to set up in Lyon.

In order to have a valid reason to set up an antenna wire across the garden of his landlord, he bought a radio set and pretended to be a law student. He immediately tried to contact the Home Station:

"Having quickly settled into my bedroom, I try to establish radio contact with England. No luck. I tune in for all my "scheds", six times a week, three times by day, three times by night. It is discouraging. Soulas, via the Polish network, tells London of my failed attempts. On June 20, the operator of the Home Station finally wakes up: the first telegrams pass in both directions.

The main qualities of the Paraset transmitter-receiver that I use are that it is both small and light. The receiver, of the reaction type, is quite sensitive and can receive weak signals, but it is a bit temperamental to set and it varies with the fluctuations of the voltage coming from the mains as well as with the proximity of the operator's hand. It can hardly be considered as selective: a powerful station, close to the wavelength of your correspondent, will burst your eardrums and makes it difficult to read Morse. The transmitter has a low power: 4 watts. On shortwave, it's not an issue, especially as my correspondent in England has sophisticated receivers and the huge antennas of the "Home Station", STS 53A, located in Grendon.

Ritually, I was also listening to the BBC on shortwave, to hear, despite the intense jamming effort of the Germans, some news about the war. Marvelous shortwave helping the weak to get the upper hand on the master race!"

The beginnings were fairly quiet: About five telegrams per week but the work intensity soon picked up.

"I had to broadcast several hours every day, sometimes up to five or six, from my bedroom in Bron (a suburb of Lyon), during daylight hours. The quartz crystals that should have allowed me to use my frequencies at night were defective.

The messages needed to go through. They did. From the age of sixteen, as a keen radio ham, I had chased rare and distant radio signals on radio sets I had manufactured. I loved this game that combines the sharpness of hearing to a taste for technical subtlety, and when in front of me I found a top-notch operator to capture a few microvolts that I had launched, sending telegrams was actually fun: the satisfaction of a job well done, plus that of a David who would be thumbing his nose at a Boche Goliath."

In order to compensate for the shortage of competent staff, the British sometimes had to fill the gaps with apprentices.

"The price to pay was a string of missed appointments, errors, dangerous and tedious repetition, - the longer the broadcast, the easier the tracking – or even dialogues of the deaf. Tempers flare, patience runs short: 'The goniometer truck is just down the street and those bastards are having tea!'

We used to send incendiary ttelegrams to the Home Station: 'I do not want to work with the operator I communicated with on August 2, his signals are unreadable!' - 'Yesterday's operator was unable to differentiate between numbers 2, 3 and 4...'

Moulin was getting impatient: 'Would you ask the Brits if, by any chance, they are not having a laugh at our expense?'

On the other side, they were not happy either: 'Shorten your broadcasts, they are way too long. We remind you that Eel should not get in contact with us every day and that his broadcasts should not last more than one hour...'

They were not wrong: we had moved from the principle, taught in training in England, of half an hour three times a week to a practice of several hours, every day. I tried to protest against those that were overwhelming me with telegrams. 'It must reach the other side!'."

"A close call!

One day in October, around 1700, while I was transmitting and as I was shifting to the receiving mode after having sent a telegram to Home Station, I heard it reporting that it could not hear me anymore. The propagation was terrible.

The propagation of short waves is completely random. We could generally rely on it to cover a certain distance if you carefully selected both the time and the wavelength. But occasionally a unique phenomenon - aurora, sunspots, magnetic storms, etc. - could suddenly change everything.

The training we had received in the UK ordered me to always broadcast as if I was a commercial radio station. Usually respectful of these rules, I should have, since broadcasting was no longer possible, sent the signal: QRT from WNG, and close the station. Was I becoming lazy? Did I develop a sixth sense? On that day I sent nothing.

Once the Paraset was stored, and hidden on top of a wardrobe - as I had been taught to do at signals school – I moved the antenna to the portable radio which I used as an alibi, and which gave me a bit of music, and then I laid on my bed with a book in hand.

The thumps of angry, rushed feet down the stairs. Somebody banged on the door, which opened violently. 'Police! Hands up!' *A dozen men, pistol in hand, entered the bedroom. It was like being in a film. Obviously they seemed surprised to only have a kid standing in front of them. It was obvious I had only just jumped from my bed and I still had my book in hand at the top of my raised arms. With my smiling face, I looked younger than the 18 years indicated on my identity card. They searched the room, they searched me, they leafed through books, looked under the bed, under the mattress, under the cabinet in the closet...*

Their faces told a story: this time, they had hit the wrong spot. Most seemed of German origin, but some were French. A grey-eyed Boche kept me under a constant gaze. I really did not look at all like a spy, with my short pants, my long neck and my good willing smile:

'What are you looking for? Perhaps I could help you?' *One of them found a paper on my desk.* 'Ach! What is it, sir? - Well, uh, you see, is the list of radio stations with the time where they broadcast the news. There, Radio Paris, Switzerland Romande, Stuttgart, BBC...' *But they were after a bigger fish than an English radio listener. After a last glance, they were gone. If I was new to this game, so were they too. That is what I thought when I realized I had left a crystal quartz - used to stabilize the transmission on its frequency - on my desk when I had packed my radio set away. This small black parallelepiped could have betrayed me but the policemen just did not see it. Sitting on the bed, I started to shake uncontrollably. Caught in my multiple safety rules violations, violations born of the lack of logistical support which imposed broadcasts that were far too long, too frequent, too static and with nobody to secure the perimeter, I was in fact saved by another violation of the basic rules. Had I obeyed the rule that we were supposed to give ourselves the attitude of a commercial station, I would have been caught in the act. On the street, the KWU team was actually waiting for me to emit again so as to refine the exact location of my radio set. While they waited, I was in fact packing my radio away. Had I, respecting the rule, announced the end of my broadcast, the policemen would have intervened immediately, without giving me time to hide anything. Because of this delay, the Boche had to go through and search half a dozen houses along the street.*

Downstairs in the kitchen, my landlord was dealing with his own panic: he had just bought on the black market a bag of 50 kg of wheat and he thought he was the target of these gentlemen. His fear made him look guilty, so the policemen dismantled some of his furniture for good measure. Calm finally returned. I went for a walk around the neighborhood. They had gone for good. I brought the Paraset and my pistol down from the top of the cabinet. With my panniers full, I mounted my bike, never to return.

A young girl in a very special family...

Josiane Somers was born December 17, 1924 in Lens, Pas de Calais. She was the daughter of a British salesman and of a French mother who was born Marcelle George. In June 1940, although she was a good student, Josie and her family were forced to evacuate France. They embarked on a British ship and established themselves on the West coast at 82, Cavandish Road, Patchway, Bristol. Her brother, Claude, immediately joined the RAF.

Even though she was under 18, Josie lied about her age to join the Free French Air Forces *(Forces Aérienne Françaises Libres)* on August 25, 1942 under service number 70279. Assigned to the Intelligence Branch of the Air Force in Queensberry Way, she was transferred to the secretariat of the Chief of Staff of the Air in late September 1943.

On February 3, 1943, Josie filled a first information sheet for the BCRA which led her to be called in for an interview on October 27, 1943. The meeting was fruitful and on November 1, 1943, a request for her transfer to the BCRA was drafted.

The training began with initial safety training for clandestine operations carried out at the Special Training School (STS) 37b «Clubb Gorse» in Beaulieu, Hampshire from December 1943 to

Above.
The Free French Air Forces Staff canteen in London. Josie Somers, soon to be known as "Venitien" can be identified 3rd from left with other female volunteers known as the "filles de l'air" (Air Girls). The officer is General Martial Valin, commander of the FAFL since July 10, 1941 and a Companion of the Ordre de la Libération by a 7 July 1945 decree.
(Josianne Somers)

Left and opposite page, bottom right.
London-based Bureau de Renseignement et d'Action ID card number 1106 belonging to Marcelle Sommers. It was issued post Novembre 6 1943, the BRAL being then part of the DGSS (Staff Section/Service Support).

Opposite page, top left.
Direction Générale des Transmissions FFI (FFI Signals directorate) pass ("Carte de circulation") number 124 delivered to "Albanais" under the false name of Renée Marcelle Pavy. *(Josianne Somers documents)*

COMITE FRANÇAIS
de la Liberation Nationale

B. R. A. L.

GRADE acting 2nd Lieut

NOM SOMERS

PRENOMS Marcelle

Signature du Titulaire:

No. 1106

F. F. I.

Direction Générale des Transmissions

N° 124

Carte de Circulation

Nom .... P A V Y

Prénoms .... Renée Denise

Inspecteur National

CERTIFICAT PROVISOIRE D'IDENTITÉ

GOUVERNEMENT PROVISOIRE
DE LA RÉPUBLIQUE

DIRECTION GÉNÉRALE
DES SERVICES SPÉCIAUX

Nom .... Somers

Prénoms .... Marcelle

Nationalité .... Française

Né le .... 19 octobre 1897

A .... Quarbecques (P. de C.)

Fils de .... Gustave Georges

et de .... Angèle de Favennes

SIGNALEMENT

Taille 1m 62

Front .... Grand

Nez .... rectiligne

Bouche .... moyenne

Visage .... ovale

Cheveux .... bruns

EMPREINTES

Pouce gauche | Pouce droit

Le Commandant de la D.G.S.S.

Below.

From the moment she arrived in the United Kingdom in late June 1940, Josie's mother, Marcelle Somers, then aged 40 and mother of two, offered her services to General de Gaulle. The family has kept the general's reply, which had been written on July 15, 1940 from St. Stephen's House and signed by de Gaulle himself. The Free French leader used that address from June 23 to July 22, 1940, then "Free France" set up camp in 4, Carlton Gardens. Marcelle joined the BCRA as a radio operator, under the alias of "Albanais", and was inserted by a Hudson "pick-up" during Operation "Halberd" near Macon, during the night of 3 to 4 of May, 1944.

Above.

Provisional identification document of the DGSS (Direction Générale des Services Spéciaux, central directorate for special services) issued to Marcelle Somers. Notice the DGER (Direction Générale des Etudes et Recherches, general directorate for studies and researches) on the ID picture, which proves that this document was produced post 26 October 1944.

M/OG.

ST. STEPHEN'S HOUSE,
Victoria Embankment,
Westminster, S.W.I.,
Abbey 1384

Londres, le 15 Juillet 1940.

Madame,

Les sentiments que m'exprime votre lettre me sont un précieux encouragement. Je vous en remercie très chaleureusement.

J'ai pris bonne note de votre offre de service et ne manquerai pas, le cas échéant, de faire appel à votre concours.

Veuillez agréer, Madame, mes hommages respectueux.

Général de Gaulle.

Mrs. SOMERS,
185, Lodge Causeway,
Fishponds,
BRISTOL, 5.-

Top.
Free French Forces (FFL) metal insignia worn by Josiane Somers.

Above.
Envelop sent to Private Josiane Somers, 22 Roland Gardens, London.
(Josianne Somers documents)

B.R.A.L.
Le Chef de la Section E.M/S
Le Chef de la
Sous-Section
ADMINISTRATIVE

Above.
Josiane in civilian clothes in London.

Top.
Josiane Somers and her mother with a soldier belonging to the Free French Forces in London. Notice how Josiane's mother has pinned a FAFL badge to her hat!

Below.
Josiane Somers as a young Free French Air Force (FAFL) volunteer.
(Josiane Somers)

January 2, 1944. Josie then underwent a period of counter-espionage training from January 9 to January 29. Between January 30 and February 6, she undertook a Para course at Ringway near Manchester (STS 51). There, she only jumped twice, probably because of inclement weather. On February 2, 1944, the alias VENITIEN was given to her. During the month of February, she first followed the «Preliminary Morse Training» course at Gumley Hall in Leicestershire (STS 41), which was then followed by the clandestine radio operator's course, which took place from March 4 to May 26, 1944 in Thame Park in Oxfordshire (STS 52). She was trained in the use of the following radio sets: A Mk III, B Mk II, Mk III * and A MCR1. On the very same day she finished the course, Venetian was selected for a mission into occupied France and forged identity documents were printed for her under the name of Jeanne ROGER.

On June 8, 1944 Lieutenant Daniel Cordier briefed her. On June 15 her forged documents were issued. Josie Somers AKA Venetian was ready! On July 6 she was taken to an American base in Harrington. She took off in a B 24 H serial number 42-50377 A which was piloted by 1st Lt. William T. ALFORD belonging to the 467th Bomber Group, 788 Bomber Squadron. Mission No. 909 bore the RAF code of «Percy 7F».

During that night Josie was parachuted with Jean Sebilleau alias Serfouette, a BCRA saboteur, on the «Negus» DZ located near Blanc, in the Indre departement. Assigned to Lieutenant Claude GROS alias «Adiabatic,» a safe house was found for Josie in the «Moulin aux Moines», an estate belonging to Mademoiselle de Harambure. A former air force academy graduate, Claude Gros had been parachuted from England on June 18, 1944 on the «Aglae» DZ also in the Indre departement. His mission was to be the operation officer for the B2 region (Charente, Deux-Sevres and Vienne departements) in order to create a parachute and air operations control network.

On July 9, Venitien moved to the Chateau de Marigny and finally settled in a small farm named "La Grenouille" («The Frog») near the Creuse River on the Chambon borough. From July 21 to 26 the radio transmissions were done from the Moulin aux Moines and from La Grenouille. It was a period of uncertainties as reflected by this report by Claude Gros, operations officer for region B2, dated November 3, 1944.

This young girl is extremely young (19 years 8 months) but she has proved to be an elite volunteer. She has an absolutely extraordinary coolness which was immediately noticed when she was operating in support of the Maquis. Despite having to, on three separate occasions, do emergency evacuation of houses from which she was operating because they had been compromised, she never ceased to maintain her composure and was always energetic. She was confronted with numerous technical problems since my frequent changes of command post location forced us to carry all the radio equipment in several different trips. She only was able to start operating in decent conditions from August 1.

Above.
A Free French Naval Force (FNFL) insignia belonging to Josiane Somers.

Top right.
Josiane Somers' Free French Air Force (FAFL) insignia.

Opposite page, top.
Provisional driving licence delivered to Josiane Somers in the UK. It was valid from 3 October 1943 to 4 October 1944...

Next page, right center.
Silk "One time pad" used for encoding messages belonging to Josiane Somers aka Venitien.
(Josiane Somers)

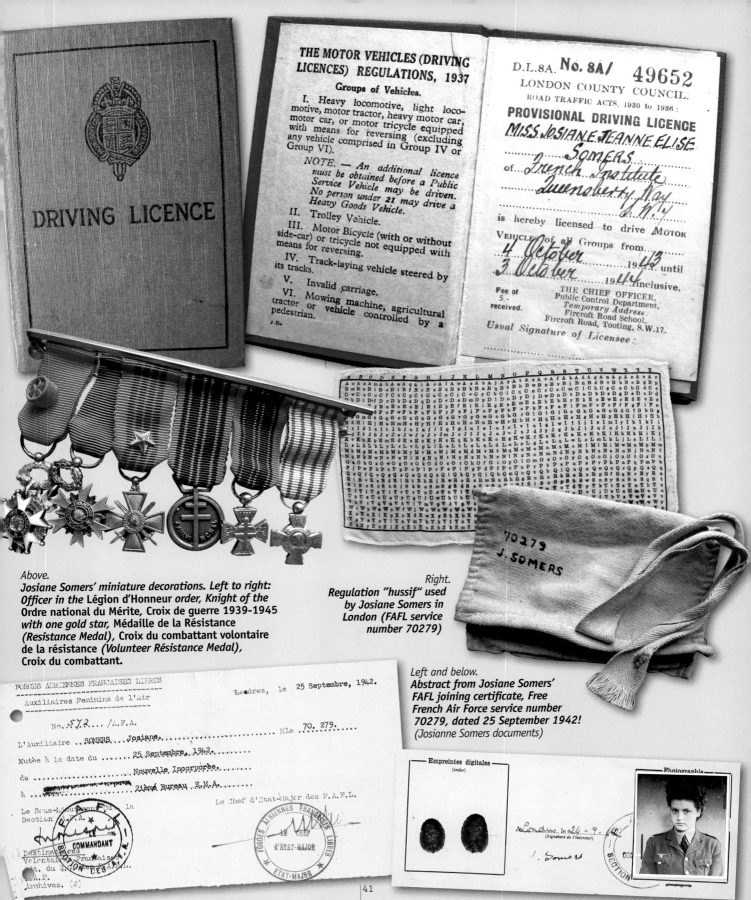

DRIVING LICENCE

THE MOTOR VEHICLES (DRIVING LICENCES) REGULATIONS, 1937

Groups of Vehicles.

I. Heavy locomotive, light locomotive, motor tractor, heavy motor car, motor car, or motor tricycle equipped with means for reversing (excluding any vehicle comprised in Group IV or Group VI).

NOTE.— An additional licence must be obtained before a Public Service Vehicle may be driven. No person under 21 may drive a Heavy Goods Vehicle.

II. Trolley Vehicle.

III. Motor Bicycle (with or without side-car) or tricycle not equipped with means for reversing.

IV. Track-laying vehicle steered by its tracks.

V. Invalid carriage.

VI. Mowing machine, agricultural tractor or vehicle controlled by a pedestrian.

J.D.

D.L.8A. **No. 8A/ 49652**
LONDON COUNTY COUNCIL.
ROAD TRAFFIC ACTS, 1930 to 1936 :

PROVISIONAL DRIVING LICENCE

MISS JOSIANE JEANNE ELISE SOMERS
of French Institute
Queensberry Way S.W.7

is hereby licensed to drive MOTOR

VEHICLES of all Groups from 4 October 1943 until
3 October 1944 inclusive.

Fee of 5 - received.

THE CHIEF OFFICER,
Public Control Department.
Temporary Address
Fircroft Road School,
Fircroft Road, Tooting, S.W.17.

Usual Signature of Licensee :

Above.
Josiane Somers' miniature decorations. Left to right: Officer in the Légion d'Honneur order, Knight of the Ordre national du Mérite, Croix de guerre 1939-1945 with one gold star, Médaille de la Résistance (Resistance Medal), Croix du combattant volontaire de la résistance (Volunteer Résistance Medal), Croix du combattant.

Right.
Regulation "hussif" used by Josiane Somers in London (FAFL service number 70279)

70279
J. SOMERS

Left and below.
Abstract from Josiane Somers' FAFL joining certificate, Free French Air Force service number 70279, dated 25 September 1942!
(Josianne Somers documents)

FORCES AERIENNES FRANCAISES LIBRES
Auxiliaires Feminins de l'Air

Londres, le 25 Septembre, 1942.

No. 572 /A.F.A.   Mle 70.279.

L'Auxiliaire SOMERS Josiane

Mutée à la date du 25 Septembre, 1942

de Nouvelle Incorporée

à 2ième Bureau E.M.A.

Le Sous-Lieutenant Fd la Section

Le Chef d'Etat-Major des F.A.F.L.

LE COMMANDANT

Destinataires
Volontaires Françaises
V. du 2ième Section DE S.A.L.
C.A.P.
Archives. (2)

LE CHEF D'ETAT-MAJOR
FORCES AERIENNES FRANCAISES LIBRES
ETAT-MAJOR

— Empreintes digitales —
(index)

Photographie

Londres, le 24-9-19...
(Signature de l'interessé)
J. Somers

The team received about twenty supply parachute drops and during the course of one of those drops Josie received a suitcase for her mother. Unbeknownst to her, her mother had also joined the BCRA. Marcelle SOMERS was also a radio operator under the alias of «Albanais». She was inserted into France by a Hudson pickup during Operation «Halberd» near Macon during the night of 3 to 4 May 1944. On October 5, 1944 Josie returned to London, mission accomplished. On October 25 she married the man who had been her operational commander while in France, Claude Gros. Her mother and father were present for the marriage but not his brother. Indeed Claude Somers still was on a mission. He also had joined the British secret service, the SOE, and also as a radio operator! He was a member of the famous Jedburgh teams with which he carried out two special missions: «Simon,» where he was landed near Les Sables d'Olonne during the night of the 27 to the 28 of September 1944 in support of the Joint Allied mission «Shinoile" and then «Dicing», a mission during which he was, on April 7 1945, parachuted South of Assen in Holland. Josie Gros-Somers passed away in June 2010.

Left.
Josiane Somers' Croix de guerre 1939-1945 with one gold star. The cross itself is of the 1939-1940 pattern.

Top left.
Claude Gros was a French Air Force officer who was posted to North Africa when the war broke out. He returned on leave to Metropolitan France on September 15, 1942 and soon escaped through Spain. Posted to the BCRA in Algiers on 1 September 1943, he followed the specific BCRA training in French North Africa. He was then posted to the United Kingdom on February 11, 1944. He was given the alias "Adiabatique" and his nom de guerre was Emile Portanière. He then received additional training for landings and parachute operations. Appointed as Operation Officer for the region B, Claude Gros was parachuted on June 18, 1944 on the "Aglaé" DZ located close to Le Blanc in the Indre département. On completion of his mission, he returned to London on October 5, 1944.
(Josiane Somers)

Left.
Sergeant Claude Somers, alias "Stéphane", Josiane Somers' brother was a Jedburgh wireless operator for the British Armed Forces. Notice how he wore his SF badge on his chest over the right pocket. The various badges on his right sleeve show that he was a Sergeant in the RAF with stripes denoting 4 years of accumulated service.
(Josiane Somers)

Below.
The crew which inserted Venitien and Serfouette seen here in in Wendover, Utah on 15 January 1944 when it belonged to 467th Bombardment Group. *Left to right, front row:* Samie Taylor, Arcade J. Boiselle, Robert Hartman, Steve Korpash, Harry McCormick and Charles Hall. Second, pilot William T. Alford, Robert J. Tully, John J. Goulding, Russell E. Kennedy.
(Carpetebeggers)

Right.
*This artwork by Jeff Bass
depicts Virginia Hall
operating a Type 3 Mk II
radio set in July 1944 from
Le Chambon sur Lignon.
The resistance fighter who
pedals on the generator is
Edmont Lebrat. Daughter
of a wealthy family from
Baltimore, Virginia Hall was
groomed for a diplomatic
career when on December 8,
1933 a hunting accident
cost her the lower left leg
and ruined all her hopes.
Having joined the French
Army in June 1940, she
then fled to London.
Recruited by the SOE, she
was sent to France posing
as a journalist. She rapidly
played a pivotal role for the
SOE in France but she had
to be exfiltrated through
Spain in 1942. At the age
of 38, she was given the
authorization by the SOE
to follow a radio operator
course at the STS 52 school
in January 44. After having
contacted the US special
services, she was admitted
into the OSS on March
10, 1943. Designated
under the alias of "Diane"
as the radio operator of
the "Saint" mission, she
was infiltrated by sea
into Brittany with her
commander Henry Laussucq
alias "Aramis" on the night
of 21 to 22 March 1944.
In May they went separate
ways and Diane started
operating from the region
of Cosne sur Loire. By mid-
June 1944, she was made
responsible for "Heckler"
mission in the Haute
Loire with the mission of
coordinating operations
with FFI groups. Around
10 July 44, she settled
around Le Chambon sur
Lignon. Virginia Hall passed
away on July 8, 1982.*
(CIA Museum, Washington)

THE RADIO SETS:
BRITISH MADE RADIO SETS

INITIALLY, INTELLIGENCE SERVICE radio sets were used (Mk V, Mk VI, Mk VII, Mk XIV, Mk XV and Mk XVI) but soon the SOE created its own research and development unit, "Station IX", which incorporated a special Signal department. It was situated in a country house near Welwyn and nicknamed "The Frythe". Directed by a Signal Corps officer (Lieutenant then Major) John I Brown (1917-1993), this Department created many radio sets, from the MCR 1 "Biscuit" to the Type B MK II Suitcase Radio. It also designed the Type A MK III, which was to become the lightest and smallest Suitcase Radio of the SOE, and which used miniaturized parts imported from the United States.

Above.
Paraset radio set used by a Norwegian underground fighter.
(Norwegian Armed Forces Museum)

Above.
John Brown (1917-1993), a British Army Royal Corps of Signals officer who was posted in 1941 to the secret SOE laboratory. He designed several radio sets for the SOE among which the famous MCR 1 "Biscuits", the Type B MK II Suitcase radio and the Type A MK III (the SOE's smallest and lightest Suitcase radio)
(MoD)

Opposite page.
Brochart alias "Charot" and Lartalias "Tral" in Amiens, Mission Sussex Drolot. Parachuted during the night of the 8th to the 9th of April 1944 in Neuvy-Pailloux (Indre département), they emitted with a Mark VII Paraset from a garage located in the city of Amiens
(picture origin unknown, Jacqueline Guillebaud presentation to the Sussex Museum)

The badge of the Sussex network. This enameled badge is in the shape of a modern French shield. It depicts a parachute holding a cross of Lorr
superimpose on a raised French flag. On both sides partial representation of the American and British national flags can be seen. The title Sussex 1
is printed on a black enamel background. The three national flags symbolize the tripartite mission involving the three secret services BCRA (France),
(USA), MIS (UK). The cross of Lorraine is a reminder that the French agents belonged to the Free French BCRA. The black colour reminds that the ag
landed in France at night. About 120 such badges were manufactured. 101 badges were numbered for the 101 agents who did operational ju
The order of numbers corresponds to the order in which the jumps were carried out.Twenty non-numbered badges were saved for some of the British
American cadre as well as for crewmembers of of the Sussex squadron. The badge was designed by Guy Wingate but produced by a manufacturer loc

The MK VII Paraset

The main qualities of a radio set are that it should be small and light. On a reaction-type receiver, the receiver part is sensitive and can receive weak signals but tuning it was always difficult. It changed with voltage variations of the mains and with the proximity of the operator's hand. It is also not very selective: a powerful station close to the wavelength of the receiving station could easily

Above.
A wireless operator at work with the Maquis. The MCR1 receiver is much in evidence as well as the mains adapter and the Type 3 Mk II emitter held in a "Para" type metal box. *(Roger Flamand)*

Previous page.
Pictured during Mission Sussex Madeleine, Lieutenant Daniel Pomeranz alias "Piron" who was parachuted on 2 June 1944 during Operation "Cord1" in Savenières near Rochefort sur Loire. Notice the Suitcase of his Mark 7 Il on the back of his bicycle. *(Sussex Museum)*

Right.
16 of June 1944 on the Dingson base in Saint Marcel. Radio team Pierre 2 belonging to 4 SAS poses for posterity in front of a "B2" suitcase and a MCR1 radio set. Jean Paulin, left, and Alexander Charbonnier right have both been among the first Troopers parachuted during the night of 5 to 6 June 1944.
(Book "Les Parachutistes SAS de la France libre", David Portier, Nimrod editions)

During the "Bataille du Vercors", Résistance fighters listen to the news bulletins thanks to their MCR1 "Biscuit" receiver. Still taken from "Au cœur de l'orage" a film by Jean-Paul le Chanois which was partially shot during the Battle for the Vercors and finally edited in 1945.

damage the eardrums of the operator and make it difficult to hear Morse. The emitter had quite a weak power (4 Watts), which is not a major inconvenience for short wavelengths.

The MCR.1 receiver "Biscuit"

One of the most famous set is the MCR.1 receiver (Miniature Communication Receiver) called the Midget which was produced under contract by the Philco Company in Perivale. At the end of the war, Philco had manufactured over 30,000 sets. They were nicknamed "biscuit sets" as they were wrapped up in Huntley and Palmer 2 pounds biscuit boxes. It could use, in an emergency, power from the mains, or it operated from dry cell batteries. It covered a frequency scale ranging from 150 Khz to 15 Mhz. Initially, it was designed to receive ordinary radio broadcasts but it was considered wiser to also cover the Morse code range.

As archaic as it may seem in 2010, it must not be forgotten that at the time the radio operated with radio tubes, or "valves", which even when miniaturized, still remained quite bulky and used up a lot of energy. In comparison, the sets issued to the British Army at the time operated from a car battery and weighed approximately 15 kilos. The MCR.1 were parachuted in large quantities in 1944, almost one for each operational landing strip. The Allied Staff feared that because of aerial bombing or sabotage operations, the mains would be cut off and that it would be impossible to listen to BBC broadcasts making it therefore impossible to carry out parachute drops and landings when they were going to be the most necessary.

The Type B3 Mk II (The famous "B2" Suitcase Radio)

Produced by the Stonebridge Park SOE factory, the B2 was a suitcase radio which included four com-

48

ponents: an emitter the frequencies of which were given by quartz crystals, a receiver, a power adapter for the alternating electrical current found in most cities or for the continuous electrical current used by batteries and a compartment dedicated to accessories: headphones, wire antenna…). The ruggedness and the dependability of those radio sets were legendary.

The Jed-Set

With the advent of the Jedburgh Teams, it soon became necessary to develop radio equipment adapted to the needs of that unit. At this time, most agents used radio sets that depended on electrical power, which either came from the mains or from batteries. However, for obvious reasons, the Jedburghs could not be relying on the mains and they could not either carry heavy and cumbersome car batteries with them. It was thus necessary to develop an independent power

Above.
**RCD 31/1 "Sweetheart" set
with headset.**
(Picture François Dujardin)

Previous page, bottom left.
A .32 ACP (7,65 mm) Colt 1903 pistol.
(Bruno Barthelot)

Top.
**In the film, "Félix", the head of the
network, receives a second wireless
operator who uses a B2 suitcase radio.**
(Now it can be told document)

supply such as a hand-cranked generator; Brown's latest invention was therefore kept.

The Type 45/III hand-cranked generator was placed on a telescopic tripod and if it worked beautifully with the B2 emitter, it proved more temperamental with the receiver. One solution was to link it up with the MCR.1. "Biscuit" set. As such, this radio set was known as the "Jed – Set" Type 46/1 (Nicholls Set with a Type 48/1 transceiver). Two Web canvas pouches could be fitted either sides of the rucksack; one was for the tripod and the other for the collapsible aerial mast. Even though these equipments were fairly heavy (17 kg for the Jed-Set and 20 Kg for the Nicholls Set), they offered the Jedburghs Teams complete autonomy in their communications with London and thus afforded them a total freedom of action.

Type 31/1 Receiver "Sweetheart"

This receiver was developed for Western Europe where BBC reception was reasonably good. It was

Opposite page.
Milton Hall, the "Daniel" Jedburgh poses for a film directed by John Ford. In the foreground, British Major Kemys D BENNANDT, "Apôtre", operates a 45/III generator while French Lieutenant Albert de Schonen, "Argentier", hands the message sheets to British radio operator Sergeant Ronald Brierley, "Florin". This team was parachuted on 4 August 1944 on DZ "Bonaparte" near Kerien (close to the town of Saint Brieuc in Brittany). After returning to London, the team was once again infiltrated in France in the night of the 4th to the 5th of September 1944, this time by a Dakota Pickup, during "Operation Mixer", near Gex in the Ain département. (Bertrand Souquet collection)

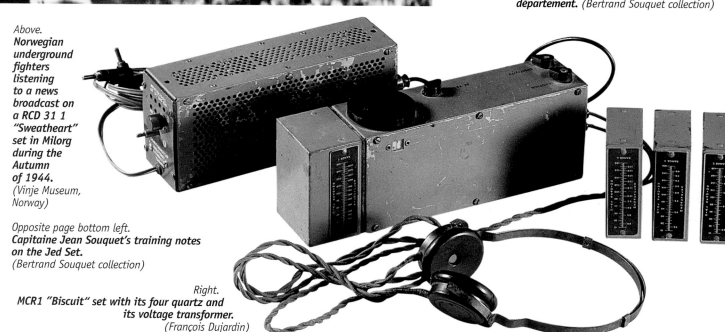

Above.
Norwegian underground fighters listening to a news broadcast on a RCD 31 1 "Sweatheart" set in Milorg during the Autumn of 1944.
(Vinje Museum, Norway)

Opposite page bottom left.
Capitaine Jean Souquet's training notes on the Jed Set.
(Bertrand Souquet collection)

Right.
MCR1 "Biscuit" set with its four quartz and its voltage transformer.
(François Dujardin)

designed by a Norwegian electronics engineer named Willy Simonsen. He arrived in the UK in 1942. Thanks to his previous service in the Norwegian Underground, he knew what clandestine operators needed and he offered his services to the War Office. He immediately started working and soon designed this radio set, which only cost £ 8 to produce. Over 50,000 were produced, 5,000 of which being bought by the Norwegian Government in exile. Its "Sweetheart" nickname is rumoured to have been linked to a pretty young British girl who was then working in Simonsen's laboratory.

This set was one of the two miniaturized sets that were parachute dropped and that were to only be used in the "receive" mode. It allowed agents belonging to the BOA or the SAP that were permanently on the move to listen to " Broadcast " messages (those messages, broadcasted on the BBC, were short coded sentences that announced parachute drops).

On 12 and 13 July 2008, during the "Résistances" commemorative events organised in the Vercors region of France, a B2 Suitcase Radio and a Mk VII Paraset were authorized to broadcast again more than 60 years

(continued on page 57)

Previous page, top.
HST 40 6V 5A Hand cranked generator in use in a Greek resistance movement.
(IWM HU-67330)

Previous page, bottom.
Norwegian underground fighters listening to a news broadcast on a RCD 31 1 "Sweatheart" set while they are being chased by the German forces during Operation "Chasewater" in April 1945.
(Oslo Resistance Museum)

Above.
Radio operators in a Home Station. It is possible to make out on the black board that some Out Stations (Jedburgh Teams Gilbert, Jeremy, Alfred and Arthur) have sent signals at 1354 GMT while others (Jedburgh Teams Hugh, Jude, Anthony and Bruce) went on the air at 1400 GMT.
(National Archives)

Right.
Female radio operators in a Home Station. *(National Archives)*

German Direction Finding

Above and page 56 top.
**View from the inside of a
Gestapo DF goniometer truck.**

*Opposite page top,
and page 56 bottom.*
**A Peugeot 201 hard top
delivery van with a ZA3
licence plate identifying it
as having been registered in
the Vaucluse département
in 1936. The roof baggage
holder hides the antenna.**

Opposite page, bottom.
**View from the inside
of another Gestapo DF
goniometer truck.**
(Now it can be told pictures)

The Germans had a special unit dedicated to the detection of clandestine emissions. It was called the Sonderkommando Kurzwellenüberwachung or KWU. DONAR was the codename of the operation. In the Walhalla, Donar is the god of thunder. He was to become the patron saint of the hunt for clandestine radios. A total of one hundred and six men, seven mobile goniometers mounted either on trucks or on one of the service's 35 cars was made available.

Close protection for those teams was provided by inspectors of the Sureté Nationale (French National Security). A control station equipped with over 300 receivers continuously monitored over thirty thousands frequencies comprised between 10 kcl s and 30 mcl s.These ultra-modern receivers provided an instant snapshot of all existing radio traffic on a 100 kcls bandwidth: each station appeared as a bright spot. Each operator had the list of the frequencies used by radio stations operating either under German control or from outside the country. Thus, any spot which appeared suddenly outside previously registered and identified frequencies

was highly likely to signal a covert radio operator. Once detected, the frequency was immediately communicated by telephone to the three direction-finding centers located in the cities of Brest Augsburg and Nuremberg.

Each of those DF center would then take a very accurate bearing in order to determine a 20X20X20 km triangle. The mobile regional base was put on alert and immediately sent two DF vehicles as well as armed detachments to the area of detection. In the DF vehicles, the receivers were tuned in to the frequency of the clandestine radio set. The vehicles would then head for the tip of the triangle, then lie in wait while keeping in contact with the other teams as well as with the control station. When the suspected area had been narrowed to a 200-metres triangle by the Mercedes DF trucks supported by an innocuous looking delivery van the back of which was covered with a tarpaulin, a few harmless looking pedestrians dressed in ample trench coats covering what seemed to be generous and reassuring paunches entered the scene. These passers-by seemed to be late and in a

hurry, engrossed in the contemplation of their wristwatches. Their paunches in fact hid a very sensitive magnetometer and the dial of the wristwatch was a measuring device the pointer of which indicating the Gestapo agent whether he was getting nearer the source of the emission or not.

Each of those agents was followed by two or three men who always kept one hand in their pocket. Suddenly, an agent would rush into a building, the men behind him would follow suit, a car would stop on the curb ... the radio operator was lost. If he had time to swallow his poison pill, the removal of the body would be very discreet ; if the neighbours had heard anything, they would be told that somebody had been arrested for a black market related offense; if shots were fired, the next day, a few lines in the newspaper would report the death of a dangerous criminal who had fired at the police when it had come to arrest him.

This was the procedure used in 1943. If the clandestine transmitter was located in the same city as a mobile goniometer base, the location of the transmitter could be identified within a 200-metres radius in less than a quarter of an hour.

As an example, the German DF could be within sight of a transmitter half an hour after it sent its very first signal. It is likely that by the spring of 1944, the Germans were using a fully automated, car-mounted DF system using a cathodic screen monitor.

With the latter system, it is likely that the transmission of an "acknowledge" message to the control, lasting a mere three seconds, would have produced a bearing with a tolerance of approximately 5 seconds, which would have given a location in a circle with a radius of less than one kilometer radius.

Analysis of the number of F section radio operators whose capture can be solely attributed to German direction finding (based on a grand total of roughly one hundred networks).

For ten arrested radio operators, at least five fell victims to carelessness of breaches of basic security rules ; another two arrest could have been avoided had the transmissions not been sent from cities where German DF teams had regional branches. Many radio operators like other members of resistance networks were compromised because of careless talks, gossip, indiscretions, police investigations or sheer bad luck in the form of a routine police check. On the other end, the fact that ten radio operators were captured should not hide the extraordinary usefulness and effectiveness of the remaining ninety if one is only to mention F section. «Kléber», belonging to the French intelligence branch and not to the SOE, never had a single incident when it used its eight transmitters to send signals to Algiers from the immediate vicinity of Pau (SW France). By 1944, the average duration of a transmission was less than three minutes per frequency.

after the end of the war. With the assistance of Pascal F8jzr, a keen radio ham and a confirmed Morse code operator and thanks to the Espace Ferrié - Musée des Transmissions de Rennes (French Army Corps of Signals Museum located in Rennes, Brittany) in cooperation with the Amicale Transmission de la Cote d'Azur (Old comrades of the French armed forces Signal Corps association from the Riviera area), using the TM4FFI call sign, the two radio sets managed to exchange over 60 messages in Morse code throughout Europe, including two messages with another radio ham and collector of clandestine radio equipments located in Alsace, East of France who was also operating WW2-era radio sets! Those broadcasts were authenticated by a dedicated QSL card, which was sent to all the contacts!

The power generators

If the Suitcase radios were generally provided with an adaptor for the mains as well as an electrical socket allowing it to be connected to any household lamp, the SOE developed a whole range of generators able to produce power in the middle of nowhere, allowing the radio operator to keep on emitting even when the Germans switched off the mains in order to locate a point of emission.

- the C Mk I hand-cranked generator, (20 watts, 6-8 volts, 3 A)
- the Bicycle compatible generator
- the Pedal powered generator (with a seat for the operator)
- the Steam ALCO steam generator
- the RB8 petrol generator

The " Heayberd " rectifier was often associated with those generators.

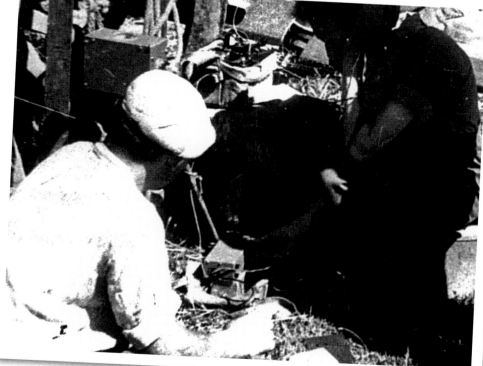

Top right.
Norwegian underground fighters listening to a news broadcast on a RCD 31 1 "Sweatheart" set in Milorg during the Autumn of 1944.
(Oslo Resistance Museum)

Right.
A Jed Set in operation during the Aloes mission in Britanny in 1944. The MCR1 "Biscuit" receiver is plainly visible on the ground as well as the 45/III Generator on its tripod and the 46/1 emitter in its canvas web pouch on the right.
(Roger Flamand)

THE AMERICAN RADIO SETS

AT THE BEGINNING OF THE WAR, the USA had no intelligence service to speak of. They had to build everything from scratch. The formidable American industry set itself in motion and quickly started producing some good quality radio sets that were characterized by their modern conception thanks to the use of techniques such as stamped sheet metal or plastic moulding. For this reason, sets such as the RCA BP-10 or the RBZ look like they were produced in the 1970s.

The American household portable receivers

The Musée de l'Ordre de la Libération (The Order of Liberation Museum in Paris, France) has on its displays two American receivers used to receive BBC broadcasts messages during clandestine air operations.

Bottom right.
Jacques Brunschwig (1905 - 1977), a former pupil from the prestigious Ecole Polytechnique was recruited early 1942 by Emmanuel d'Astier and quickly given important functions within the Libération-sud resistance movement. Arrested by the French police on 1 May 1942, Jacques Brunschwig was interned in Marseille in the Fort Saint-Nicolas. Released on 19 May, he resumed his activities (organization of strikes, sabotage, demonstrations ...). In late 1942, he left the South of France and joined the Libération-nord movement which had been founded by Christian Pineau in the occupied zone. In October 1943, Jacques Brunschwig flew to England only to return to France on 31 March 1944 when he was parachuted onto the "Dentelle" DZ near Saint-Aignan. He was arrested by the Gestapo on June 20, 1944 under the identity of Bordier and tortured. He was then detained in the Fresnes prison in Paris. On August 15, 1944 he was deported to Buchenwald concentration camp, then to Dora and finally to the Buchenwald kommando of the Nordhausen camp. During the night of the 3 to the 4 of April 1945, with two friends, he took advantage of a bombardment to escape. One of the escapees was soon killed but the two survivors managed to link up with American troops on April 8. Jacques Brunschwig was made a Companion of the Ordre de la Libération by a November 17, 1945 decree. (Musée de l'Ordre de la Libération collection)

The RCA BP-10, which was produced in 1940, looks very modern with its Bakelite casing, its chromed surfaces and its compactness (22 x 9 x 7,6 cm). The Emerson 455, produced in 1942, has a similar size but its design, complete with Ingraham-style wooden casing, is more in tune with its times. One should keep in mind that even if those sets were household sets, the mere fact of owning, in a German-occupied territory, a US-made radio set produced after the beginning of the war could have led to very dire consequences for the owner of the said set.

The Issued American radio sets

As early as 1942, the SSTR-1 transceiver was of the super heterodyne type (meaning that the Morse key could not be heard, even in a building were other people could be listening to the wireless). This was an appreciable bonus as the reaction sets could generate disturbances in neighbouring wireless sets. Interestingly, in 1947, when French

Above, previous page bottom.
American Emerson 455 receiver used by Major Jacques Brunschwig-Bordier when he was dropped near Saint-Aignan on 31 March 1944 on the "Dentelle" DZ with Alix d'Unienville.
(J.-L. Perquin, Musée de l'Ordre de la Libération collection)

Previous page, top.
A still from the film "Now it can be told". Résistance fighters listen to the BBC's personal messages on an American-made, commercial range Emerson radio set hoping for the code announcing a para drop.
(Now it can be told collection)

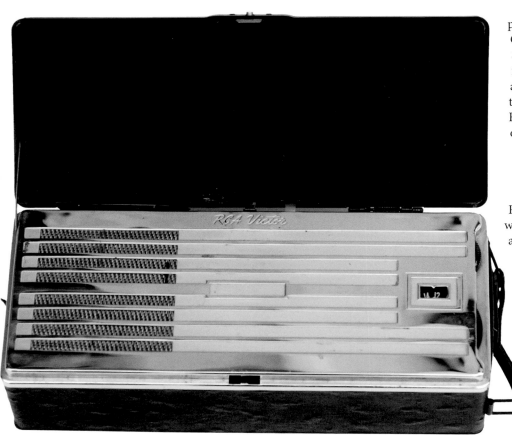

polar explorer Paul-Émile Victor went to the Groenland, his two radio operators used a SSTR1 set to establish communication from the geometrical centre of Groenland at 76° degrees North Latitude. Two operators who had served in the OSS « Penny Farthing » Lyon-based network were part of the polar expedition. They were Mario Marrand alias Rossignol or Toto (parachuted "blind" in August 1943 8 km from St Ament de Tallende, in the Puy de Dôme département, arrested 11 April 1944) and Robert Rouand, a peacetime friend of Mario who was recruited in France. The two were already qualified radio operators before the outbreak of the war.

During one his polar missions, Robert Rouand had taken his OSS-issued SSTR-1 radio set with him. This set saved his and a number of his comrades' lives when they got lost in the icy desert of the North Pole. Rouand and his friends would never have made it back if had not been for the indestructible SSTR-1…all the other sets having long broken down by this stage!

Above.
American RCA BP-10 receiver belonging to Paul Rivière alias « Marquis ».
(J.-L. Perquin, Musée de l'Ordre de la Libération collection)

Right.
Paul Rivière (1912-1998) alias: Sif bis - Galvani - Marquis — A professor of literature by profession, he was drafted in 1939 and wounded by shrapnel in Saumur on June 20, 1940. In late February 1941, he joined the National Liberation Movement (MLN). In July 1941, Paul Rivière gave up teaching to devote himself to the Resistance. With Raymond Fassin (aka Sif) who was Jean Moulin's liaison officer, he selected landing strips and dropping zones as well as potential radio emission points all over his area of responsability. On June 23, 1942, he was arrested by the Vichy police in Clermont-Ferrand for possession of forged IDs just one day after having been involved in a parachute drop. Detained in the Saint Paul prison, he was sentenced on 31 October 1942 but released on the same evening after payment of a fine. He linked up with Sif again and played a pivotal role in the Résistance by organizing radio transmission in the southern zone. Following orders given by Jean Moulin, he left France for England with Henri Frenay on June 16, 1943 as part of an air operation. After the arrest of Jean Moulin in Caluire on June 21, 1943, Rivière was no longer in a position to complete his training in the British schools. His parachute course was shortened to a mere two days and on July 21, 1943, Colonel Passy sent him back to France to replace Bruno Larat who, as the head of the Centre d'Opérations d'Atterrissages et de Parachutages (COPA, for Parachuting and Landings Operations Center) had also been arrested in Caluire. Paul Riviere was parachuted on the «Vincent» DZ, near Cormatin. He personally led 13 illegal landings including the delivery of a considerable number of agents from both London and Algiers or the delivery of funds and equipment coming from England. He was briefly recalled to London in May 1944 only to be parachuted back into France on June 7, 1944 during "Operation John 87 A" on the "Metacarpe" DZ in Soulcy close to the River Arroux, in the Saone et Loire département. Paul Rivière was made a Companion of the ordre de la Libération by a March 24, 1945 decree. (Musée de l'Ordre de la Libération collection)

THE POLISH RADIO SETS

The Type A sets were produced for a number of different resistance organisations. They had a metal casing with a black finish. In 1943, they were given the AP nomenclature code.

The Pipsztok series of radio sets dated back to the 1930s when the Polish Military Intelligence contacted the AVA Company, a small Warsaw-based factory, in order to provide its agents with radio sets.

An electronic engineer by the name of Tadeusz Heftman was put in charge of the project. The exact number of Pipsztoki (Peepshtocks) radio sets produced before the beginning of the war is not known. It is very likely that those radio sets were used by the Polish Military Intelligence in the USSR in 1939. The AVA Company was also involved in the production of the German Enigma encryption and decryption machines, thus giving the Polish authorities the opportunity to break the German codes. In September 1939, the AVA Company was evacuated first to Romania and then to France. Heftman took the blue prints of the machine as well as a prototype with him, the idea initially being to resume the production in France. The German advance put an end to that project.

Heftman still managed to make it to the British Isles and he was soon posted to the Polish radio Home Station, tasked with resuming yet again the production of the set but with British equipment. He completed the first set, the A1 "Nelka" in 1941. It was named after a pretty young girl who was then working in the Signals office of the Polish Head-quarters. A total of 23 sets was assembled in 1941 while another 183 A1 and A2 sets were produced for the SOE in 1942.

In 1943, two new sets made their appearance; the A3 (also known as the AP3) and the most popular of them all, the AP4. The AP4 outclassed all the other clandestine radio sets used by the Allies. The Polish Home Station produced 583 A1, A2, A3 and AP4 set in 1943, mostly for the SOE. Because of the limited frequency range of the early sets and because it had been determined that in order to establish a good quality radio link with occupied Poland the operators needed to work on 14 Mhz, a new set, named the AP5, was designed. A total of 122 AP5 was produced. In the final months of the war, two new types appeared, the AP6 and the AP7 receiver.

Above.
Re-enactement picture depicting a clandestine radio operator with a Polish A1 Nelka radio set *(O. Blanc-Brude picture, radio set belonging to P. Giraud of the Amicale des transmissions de la Côte d'Azur)*

ENCRYPTION TECHNIQUES

As it was of course impossible to transmit messages without encoding them, several ciphers were used throughout the war.

The Playfair code

It was the first system used in the early stages of the SOE, in 1941. It was nothing else than the cipher system used by the British Army during WWI named after Sir Hugh Lyon Playfair. A very simple system, it had the advantage of not forcing the agent to carry with him any incriminating document. All he had to do was to commit a few lines of poetry to memory. The technique encrypts pairs of letters instead of single letters as in the simple substitution cipher

Double transposition (1941-1942)

The principle of the double transposition is simple but its implementation is complex and requires time. The idea is to turn a text written horizontally into columns and to then use a numerical key. The letters were then grouped in blocks of five in order to produce a ready-to-send coded telegram.

Deciphering was done in reverse order. At the beginning of 1942, the operating procedures were that telegrams should be no shorter than 100 letters and no longer than 500; that two keys of different length should be used (10 and 12 figures, 8 and 2 etc.); to add seven to ten void letters at the beginning as well as enough void letters at the end so that the number of letters in the telegram should be a

multiple of 5 while avoiding at the same time to completely fill out the grid. Keys were changed for each message and, during the early period of the SOE, they were selected in a book, generally a non-descript novel. The agent and the Home Station would both have it in exactly the same edition. The page number, line and number of letters chosen for the two grids were indicated by the two groups placed at the beginning of the message.

This system was both tedious to use and operationally dangerous as the agent had to keep the book with him, remember the conversion tables for both letters and figures and remember as well the secret number which was used to secure the cipher. A poetry line learnt by heart quickly replaced the book. The two transposition keys were deducted from the poetry.

A-Z code

This double transposition system used keys that were prepared in advance and printed on a silk handkerchief, which was given to the agent on the day of his departure.

Two sets of keys were used. One, which was known as "Your keys to us" or "Out station to Home" was used by the agent for the messages he sent toward Home Station. The other set, known as "Our keys to you" was meant to decipher the messages sent by Home Station.

Each group of two keys was preceded by a 5-letter group placed at the beginning and at the end of the message indicating which line to chose for

deciphering. The advantages over more primitive codes were obvious. The keys were ready to use, the agent did not need to commit to memory secret number or conversion tables, thus reducing the risks of committing mistakes when using the cipher. The incriminating and cumbersome book was no longer necessary. The keys were long sequences of numbers machine-produced in a random way, which made the system even safer.

Finally, in the event the agent was to be tortured, he would have no cipher to reveal since he would not have had learnt anything by heart. On the other hand, the handkerchief was an incriminating item, which was dangerous to carry around. After ciphering a message, orders were to immediately tear out and destroy the line, which held the keys and destroy them on the spot. The idea was to make sure the enemy would not be able to decipher previously recorded messages using captured keys.

Transition systems (1942-1943)

Transition systems were used in parallel with double transposition (which was nearly extinct but which got a new lease on life with the A-Z code) between November 1942 and August 1943. Since double transposition was obsolete, all those systems had to be removed from service and replaced by substitution ciphers.

Left.
Different codes printed on either paper, see through plastic or silk all used during the Sussex mission. *(Sussex collection)*

Opposite page, bottom left.
Q code sheet of paper used during the Sussex/Vis mission, an OSS mission in the Blois area of France. Agents Vaas and Soulier were parachuted during the night of the 1st to the 2nd of June 1944 during Operation "Cord 1" in Savennières near Rochefort sur Loire in the Maine et Loire département. The Q code is an international radio brevity code.
(J.-L. Perquin)

A B C D E F G H I J K L M N O P Q R S T U V W X Y Z

Below.
Sheet of paper belonging to the emergency code Plan Arcturus of the Sussex/Vis mission.
(Etienne List Sussex collection)

PART 1.

PLAN NAME A R C T U R U S

	FIELD CALLING	FIELD FREQ.	BASE CALLS 1234567890	FIELD CALLS 1234567890
			JLVWUMESKG	IJBRYGPNLM
	OZM	-W	CWZVDAHXKT	LIBDSUEFYP
	OFP	-W	TXARHKCZVW	WGEUCJNYXL
	OPB	-W	RDEUIJSXMK	TBHFYLWVZP
	OLC	-W	VZJPMKYLWR	GAUIDTNBES
	OBF	-W	HFZMJIKXDU	RTNBPVAYLW
5.	OAH	-X	LPVWJCOYFM	KESHRTNBZA
6.	OCJ	-X	CDYFUXIJBZ	SHEMGVWRAK
7.	OGZ	-X	NPGVLAKSJT	HMEDFUXBZC
8.	OQB	-W	* FUAXKWRIYL	CHPMSJTBNZ
9.	OTC	-X	CIUWGRHEDV	AYFBTJSNZP
10.	OFW	-X	YTFBXMKLWC	SPHLRANEVU
11.	OMF	-X	XTFKRWZJGC	ABLEDNIMUY
12.	ONP	-W	VXMGPESHUC	YTJKWZRVLI
13.	OQL	-W	GTERNICDAS	UXZWMPFVY
14.	OSY	-X	MCATYLJINE	SGHKBWFT
15.	OCW	-X	CRVYPUDNEK	BXKSAFO
16.	OGU	-W	BRYGPNLMIJ	MKVNFL
17.	OVT	-X	MKRDEUIJSX	KSAFG
18.	OBL	-X	VYPUDNEKCR	YGZS
19.	OWM	-W	LEDNIMVYAB	EUC
20.	OAP	-X	ZHVAYDUTME	HKE
21.	ORZ	-X	UWIGRHEDVC	PW
22.	OTY	-X	ATYLJINEMC	
23.	OBQ	-X	ERNICDASGT	JKWZRVL
24.	OCZ	-X	YLMFTNBXRE	WCRSKIBFLJ
25.	OFV	-X	WFZGLPNJCB	XKWRIYLAFU
26.	ONG		VAAISZWKHF	DWFZIFVSCEH
27.	OEJ	-X	EDFUXBZCHM	WBUMESKOJL
28.	OPE	-X	GVLAKSJTNP	ERMDYJQOGB
29.	OLM	-W	MZKFRYAITD	
30.	OTA	-W		
31.				

1. TO MAKE
2. KEEP C
3. IF A F
CONTAINING
4. DO NOT U
5. IF YOUR
HAVE TRAFFIC.

PART 2.

PLAN NAME A R C T U R U S

ZONE	BASE MARKER FREQ	CALL	BASE FREQUENCIES (U)MAIN (A)ALT.		FIELD FREQUENCIES CALL WORKING		
B.	3208	BCA					
	3462	BCB	BM.3432	BA.3722	B.3506	BW.3302	BX.3496
	3526	BCC					
F.	4072	BCD					
	4252	BCE					
	4485	BCF	FM.4337	FA.4697	F.4517	FW.4168	FX.4303
G.	5327	BCG	GM.5582	GA.6087	G.5408	GW.5143	GX.5384
H.	6525	BCH	HM.6390	HA.6743	H.6460	HW.6631	HX.6711
I.	8215	BCI	IM.8305	IA.8445	I.8352	IW.8026	IX.8459

B/C SCHEDULE:

		TIME--DAILY
GROUP CALL -	G M W	1000 GMT .
INDIVIDUAL TFC. CALL -	X B M	2000 GMT .

INSTRUCTIONS

1. TO MAKE CONTACT USE CRYSTAL WITH SINC
2. KEEP CALLS SHORT.
3. IF A FREQUENCY CHANGE IS DESIRED, SE
CONTAINING THE INDICATOR LETTERS OF THE
4. DO NOT USE ANY SP CRYSTAL UNTIL NOT
5. IF YOUR B/C CALL APPEARS IN THE IND
HAVE TRAFFIC.

CODE " Q "

Q.R.Q..CHIFFREZ A NOUVEAU LE MESSAGE

Q.R.V..JE SUIS PRET

Q.R.V.?.ETES VOUS PRET

Q.S.Z..PASSEZ LES GROUPES DEUX FOIS

Q.T.R..DONNEZ L'HEURE

Q.T.A..ANNULEZ MESSAGE NR...

Q.R.B..JE NE SUIS PAS D'ACCORD AVEC NOMBRE DE GROUPES

Q.R.I..VOTRE NOTE VARIE

Q.S.P..PRIORITE

Q.R.M..VOUS ETES-BROUILLE PAR D'AUTRES STATION

Q.S.V..PASSEZ UNE SERIE D'APPELS

Q.S.L..J'ACCUSE RECEPTION DE VOTRE MESSAGE

Q.K..JE RECTIFIE

IMI.. INTERROGATION

A.A..TOUT APRES

A.B..TOUT AVANT

DN...BARRE DE FRACTION

Q....D'ACCORD

R.... REOU

R.P.T..REPETEZ

AS...ATTENDEZ

VA...FIN

BT...TRAIT DE SEPARATION

K...J'ECOUTE

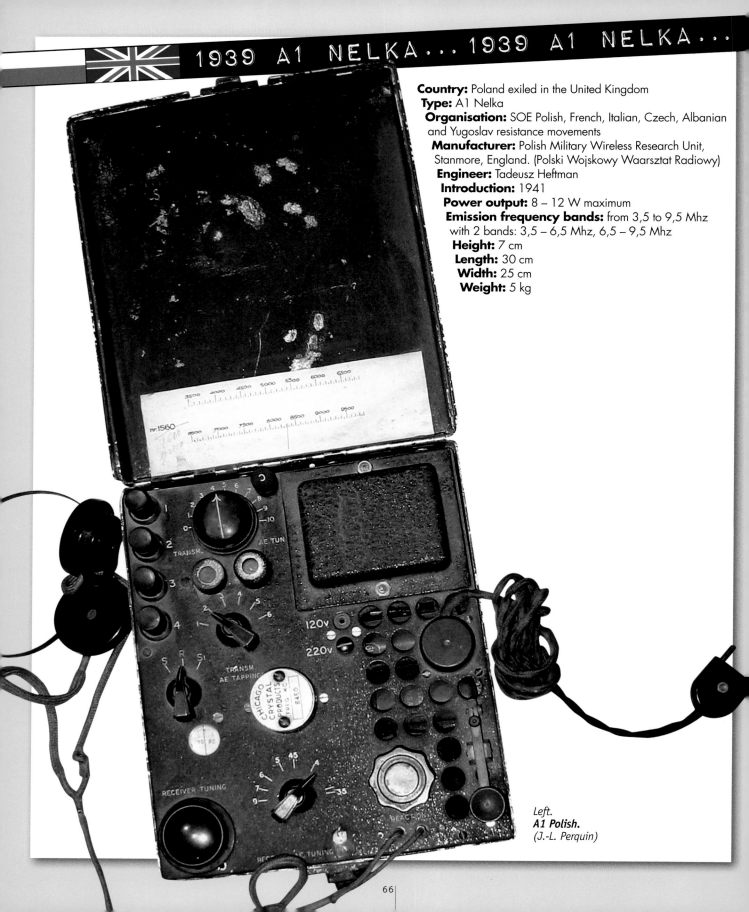

Country: Poland exiled in the United Kingdom
Type: A1 Nelka
Organisation: SOE Polish, French, Italian, Czech, Albanian and Yugoslav resistance movements
Manufacturer: Polish Military Wireless Research Unit, Stanmore, England. (Polski Wojskowy Waarsztat Radiowy)
Engineer: Tadeusz Heftman
Introduction: 1941
Power output: 8 – 12 W maximum
Emission frequency bands: from 3,5 to 9,5 Mhz with 2 bands: 3,5 – 6,5 Mhz, 6,5 – 9,5 Mhz
Height: 7 cm
Length: 30 cm
Width: 25 cm
Weight: 5 kg

Left.
A1 Polish.
(J.-L. Perquin)

Country: United Kingdom
Type: A Mk I
Organisation: SOE
Designer: Major John I. Brown
Introduction: end 1941- beginning 1942
Power output: 60 W
Emission frequency bands: 3 – 4 Mhz, 6 – 8 Mhz
Antenna length: 20 m

Receiver
height: 15 cm
length: 16 cm
width: 24 cm
weight: 2,5 kg

Transmitter
height: 15 cm
length: 16 cm
width: 24 cm
weight: 1,9 kg

Adapter
height: 15 cm
length: 16 cm
width: 10,5 cm
weight: 3,4 kg

Batteries
height: 15 cm
length: 16 cm
width: 10,5 cm
weight: 2,8 kg

Complete case
height: 17 cm
length: 32 cm
width: 44 cm
weight: 13,2 kg

Below.
A Mk I.
(J.-L. Perquin)

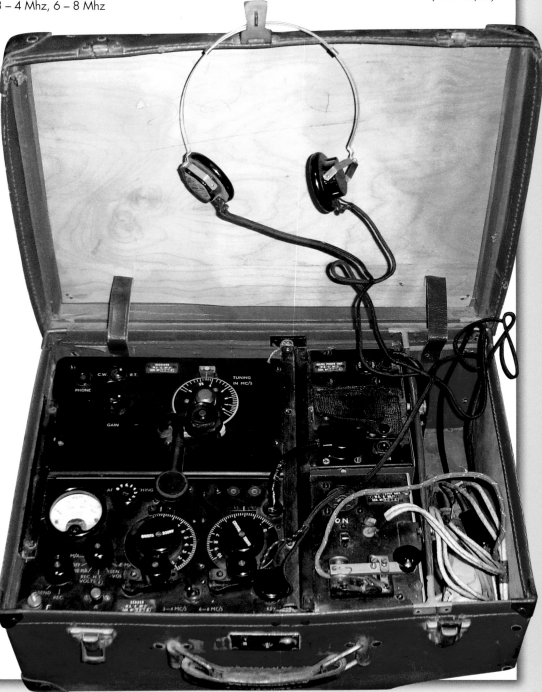

It is one of the first radio designed by the SOE; the 4 main parts were held in a metal frame within a suitcase. This set was designed to emit to a maximum range of 800 km.

Several variants were known under the following names: Type 21, A Mk I and A Mk I*, Type 21 Mk I and Type 21 Mk I*. The A Mk II is also known as Type 21 Mk II etc.

Country: United Kingdom
Type: Mk VII (Paraset)
Organisation: MI6 SIS (as well as SOE)
Manufacturer: SIS Section VIII
Introduction: 1941
Power output: 4 – 5 W
Emission frequency bands: 3,3 – 4,5 Mhz, 4,5 – 7,6 Mhz

Transmitter-receiver	Battery	Accessories
height: 11 cm	height: 11 cm	height: 11 cm
length: 14 cm	length: 11 cm	length: 11,5 cm
width: 22,5 cm	width: 14 cm	width: 14 cm
weight: 2,3 kg	weight: 2,7 kg	weight: 2,9 kg

The main/battery adapter was held in a metal case; when the box was shut nothing was visible and the entire box looked like a tin can of biscuits. A wooden box version was also produced.

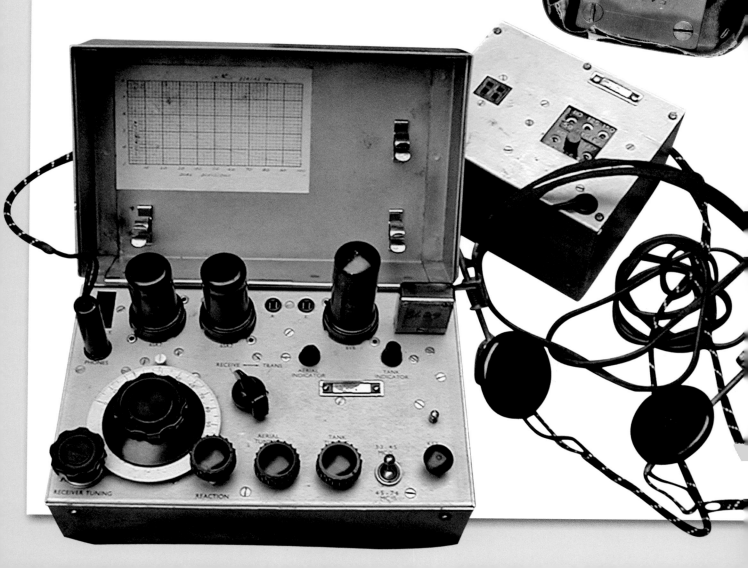

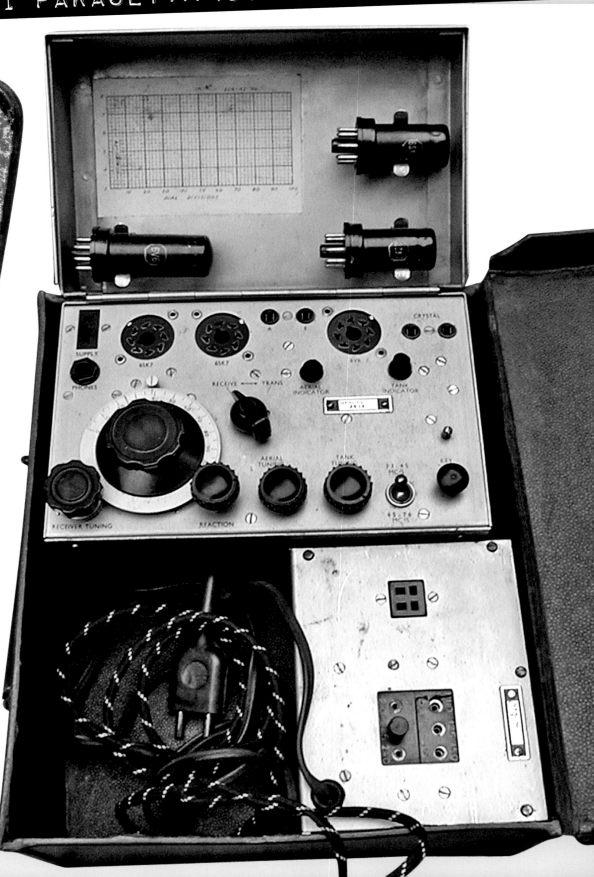

Above.
Quartz box used by the Sussex Foudre mission. Agents Leroyer and Coulon were parachuted on 7 June 1944 near Villiers-sous-Grez in the Seine et Marne département. It was an OSS mission in the city of Juvisy.

Previous page, bottom and right.
Mk VII Paraset radio with its main adapter. "Dentelle" Sussex Mission. Parachuted on 7 July 1944 on Fouilleuse.
(Etienne List Sussex collection)

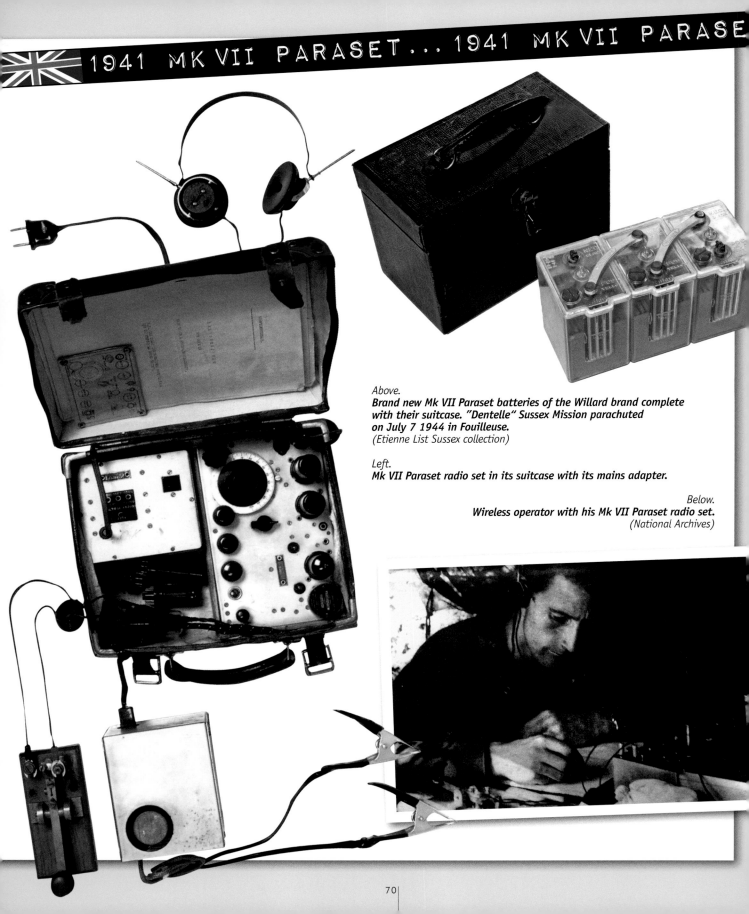

Above.
**Brand new Mk VII Paraset batteries of the Willard brand complete
with their suitcase. "Dentelle" Sussex Mission parachuted
on July 7 1944 in Fouilleuse.**
(Etienne List Sussex collection)

Left.
Mk VII Paraset radio set in its suitcase with its mains adapter.

Below.
Wireless operator with his Mk VII Paraset radio set.
(National Archives)

Left.
***Inside view
of the back side of
a Mk V set.***
*(Régis Le Mer,
CHRD Fonds Greffe
collection)*

Country: United Kingdom
Type: Mk V
Organisation: MI6, SIS, and SOE
Manufacturer: SIS Section VIII,
Whaddon Hall/Little Horwood
Introduction: 1941/1942
Power output: 25 W
Emission frequency band:
2,9 to 18 with three plugs
Receiving frequency: two plugs:
3,7 – 7,5 Mhz and 7 – 16 Mhz

The radio set was produced at
the beginning of the war. Many
versions exist including a suitcase
version.

Emitter
height: 41 cm
length: 21 cm
width: 16 cm

Right.
Mk V emitter.
*(Régis Le Mer picture, CHRD Fonds
Greffe collection)*

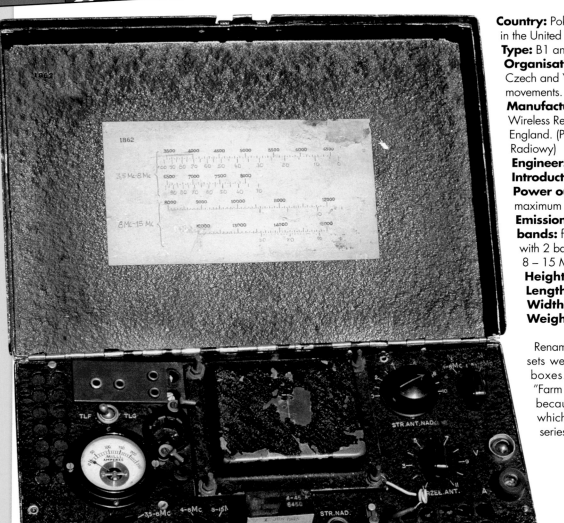

Country: Poland exiled in the United Kingdom
Type: B1 and B2
Organisation: SOE Polish, French, Czech and Yugoslav resistance movements.
Manufacturer: Polish Military Wireless Research Unit, Stanmore, England. (Polski Wojskowy Waarsztat Radiowy)
Engineer: Tadeusz Heftman
Introduction: 1942
Power output: 15-30 W maximum
Emission frequency bands: from 4 to 15 Mhz with 2 bands: 4 – 8 Mhz, 8 – 15 Mhz
Height: 25 cm
Length: 21 cm
Width: 9,5 cm
Weight: 5,5 kg

Renamed BP in 1943, those radio sets were housed in black metal boxes. They were nicknamed "Farm house set" (as in "field sets") because of their power output which was higher than the "A" series sets.

Left.
Polish B2.
(Museeradiomili collection)

Country: USA
Type: SSTR-1
Organisation: OSS
Manufacturer: Radio Development & Research Corp
Introduction: 1942
4 types of receiver: SSR-1-A, SSR-1-D, SSR-1-E and SSR-1-G
2 types of transmitter: SST-1-A et SST-1-E
Power output: more than 8-15 W
Emission frequency bands:
SST-1-A: 3 – 5 Mhz, 5 – 8 Mhz and 8 – 14 Mhz
SST-1-E: 3 – 7 Mhz, 6 – 12 Mhz and 8 – 15 Mhz
Hand cranked generator: 11,5 kg

Transmitter	Receiver	Power Supply
height: 7,6 cm	height: 10,2 cm	height: 8,9 cm
length: 24,1 cm	length: 24,1 cm	length: 24,1 cm
width: 10,2 cm	width: 7,6 cm	width: 15,2 cm
weight: 1,8 kg	weight: 2,3 kg	weight: 4,5 kg

This set was the standard American clandestine radio set, made up of three main parts held in a suit-case. It became used by the OSS from 1942 on, on the European Theater of Operations as well as in Southeast Asia.

Below.
SSTR 1 1942 American set.
(Stein Aasland)

Country: United Kingdom
Type: 3 Mk II also named Type B Mk II or simply "B"
Organisation: SOE
Designer: Major John I. Brown, station IX, The Frythe, Welwyn
Manufacturer: Radio Communication Department, SOE Stonebridge Park

Introduction: 1942
Power output: 20 W
Emission frequency bands: 3,3 – 16 Mhz with 4 quartz
L1: 3,5 – 5 Mhz   L3: 6,5 – 10 Mhz
L2: 4,5 – 7,5 Mhz   L4: 9 – 16 Mhz

This was the best-known and most sought after suitcase radio. Its power was specially appreciated. It was designed to emit at ranges over 800 km. The transmitter had a power of 15 W, which proved dangerous when operating in urban areas. On the other hand, the tuning of the suitcase was heavy and bulky and the power was such that it could create its own set of problems.

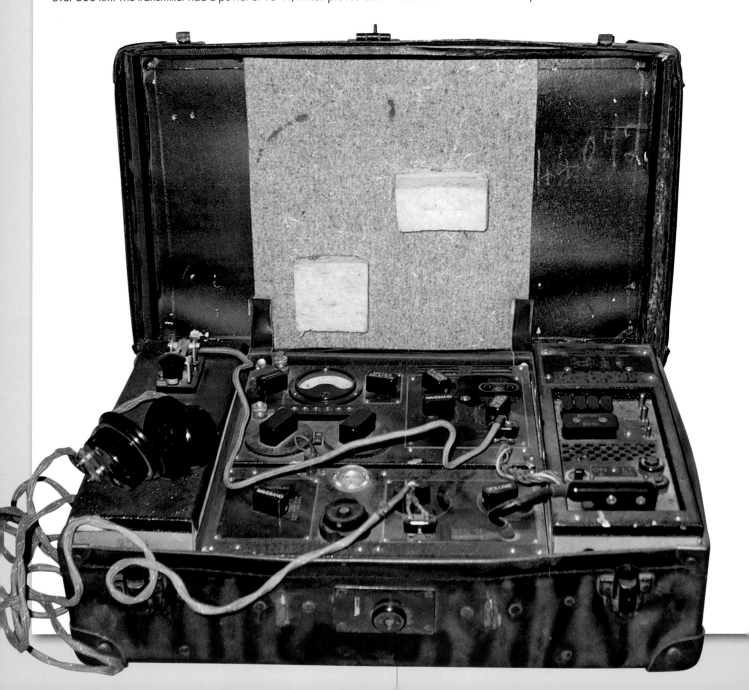

Right.
1942 Type 3 Mk II set often nicknamed "B2".
(Etienne List collection Sussex)

Previous page.
Type 3 Mk II transceiver used by Gérard Brault "Kim W" who was parachuted on 15 April 1942 near Montluçon. He was arrested on 15 October and managed to escape from the Castres prison on 29 June 1943. Back to London in July 1943, he volunteered for another mission under the alias "Sénégalais". Parachuted on 11 April 1944 in Mourmelon as part of the Citronnelle mission (a mission in support of the Ardennes maquis), he linked up with the advancing American forces in the Ardennes region on 5 September 1944.
(J-L. Perquin, Musée de l'Ordre de la libération)

Receiver
height: 12,3 cm
length: 24 cm
width: 11,5 cm
weight: 2,3 kg

Emitter
height: 12,3 cm
length: 24 cm
width: 16 cm
weight: 2,8 kg

Adapter
height: 13 cm
length: 27 cm
width: 10 cm
weight: 4,6 kg

Spare parts box
height: 13 cm
length: 27 cm
width: 8,5 cm
weight: 1,6 kg

Complete case
height: 14 cm
length: 32 cm
width: 42 cm
weight: 13,2 kg

Antenna length: 18 and 3 m

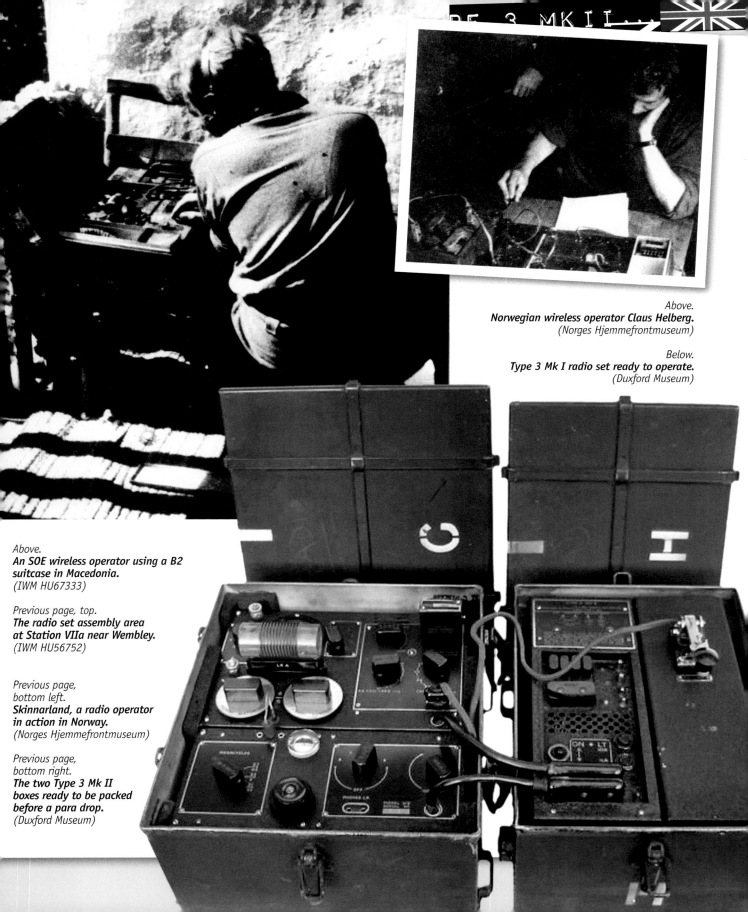

PE 3 MKII...

Above.
Norwegian wireless operator Claus Helberg.
(Norges Hjemmefrontmuseum)

Below.
Type 3 Mk I radio set ready to operate.
(Duxford Museum)

Above.
An SOE wireless operator using a B2 suitcase in Macedonia.
(IWM HU67333)

Previous page, top.
The radio set assembly area at Station VIIa near Wembley.
(IWM HU56752)

Previous page, bottom left.
Skinnarland, a radio operator in action in Norway.
(Norges Hjemmefrontmuseum)

Previous page, bottom right.
The two Type 3 Mk II boxes ready to be packed before a para drop.
(Duxford Museum)

The so-called "Para" version of the Type 3 Mk II. It was made up of two parts: type G and type H.
(J.-L. Perquin)

Country: Poland exiled
in the United Kingdom
Type: OP 3 (type 30/1)
Organisation: SOE,
Polish, French and Danish resistance
movements
Manufacturer: Polish Military
Wireless Research Unit, Stanmore,
England. (Polski Wojskowy Waarsztat
Radiowy)
Introduction: 1943
Receiving frequency: three-position
switch: 0,6 – 1,5, 2 – 5 and 5
to 12 Mhz
Height: 4 cm
Length: 17,5 cm
Width: 12,5 cm
Weight: 0,8 kg

This receiver was also known as the
30/1. Its appearance is very similar
to the 31/1 "Sweetheart" and its
main purpose was to receive the BBC's
"Broadcast" messages. The set is switched
off by unplugging the battery housing.
287 sets were produced during the war and about
105 were airdropped in Poland in the Summer of
1944. These sets were also used in other areas of
occupied Europe. They were delivered with two 1,5 V
and one 60 V battery. The battery life is estimated
to have been in the 35 to 50 hours range. The
full radio kit complete with accessories
(battery housing, batteries, headsets,
wire antenna and grounding
cable weighed 1,5 kg. A label
with the operating instructions
was positioned on one
of the sides in English,
Danish or Polish.

Above.
Polish OP 3 (type 30/1) with headset.
On top of the receiver: a label with the operating instructions in Polish. On the front, left to right: the headset plug marked by a T (Telephon), the two dials, the volume control (SILA), the grounding cable plug marked by a Z (Ziema); the frequency selector can be seen on the bottom left; at the very bottom the Gr (Grafia) control to switch to oscillation, the antenna plug marked by an A (Antenna) and finally the STR (Strojenie) frequency control switch.
(Guy Millot collection and picture).

Right.
***Inside view
of an OP 3 receiver.***
*(Guy Millot collection
and picture)*

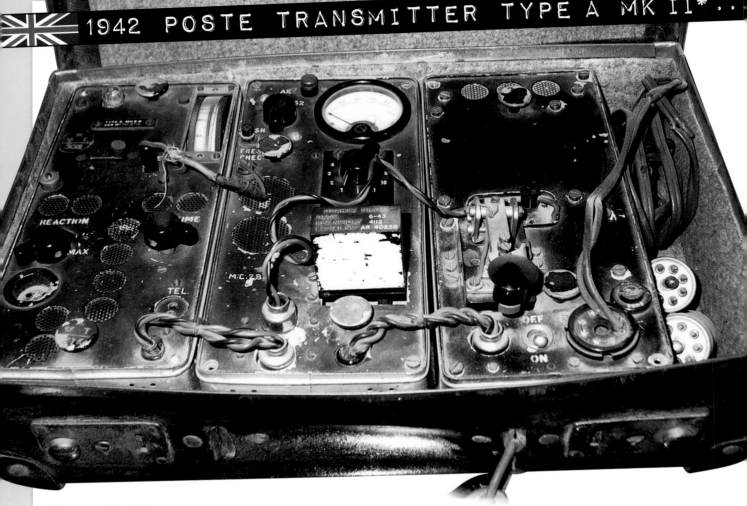

Country: United Kingdom
Type: A Mk II*
Organisation: SOE
Designer: Major John I. Brown
Manufacturer: Marconi Co
Introduction: 1942
Power output: 6 W
Frequency band: 3 – 4,5 Mhz (blue), 6 – 9 Mhz (red)
Length of the antenna: 8 m (green colour) and 3 m of grounding cable (black colour)

Receiver
height: 9 cm
lenght: 23 cm
width: 10 cm
weight: 1,6 kg

Adapter
height: 9 cm
lenght: 23 cm
width: 10 cm
weight: 3,4 kg

Batteries
height: 9 cm
lenght: 23 cm
width: 10 cm
weight: 2,4 kg

Transmitter
height: 9 cm
lenght: 23 cm
width: 10 cm
weight: 1,4 kg

Spare parts box
height: 10 cm
lenght: 23 cm
width: 7 cm

Complete suitcase
height: 12 cm
lenght: 25 cm
width: 39 cm
weight: 8,4 kg

Above.
1942 Type A MK II* set.
(J.-L. Perquin, Musée de l'Ordre de la Libération collection)

An improvement over the Type 21, A Mk I and A Mk I* radio sets, this set also had a variant named the A Mk II* or Type 21 Mk II*.

It was made up of three identical casings containing:

- a short wave receiver - from 4 to 9 Mc/s, high sensitivity – station selection was rendered easier by a good spread of the frequencies. Listening was done through a headset, which was plugged in on top of the receiver.

- a transmitter covering the same frequency bands and having an aerial output of 5 W. The transmitter was very accurate and very stable on its frequencies thanks to the use of a quartz oscillator, which was directly plugged in

on top of the casing. A miniaturized Morse key could also be plugged in the same way

- the power supply allowed for the adjustment to whatever voltage was locally available. A built-in oscillator was capable of converting the continuous electrical current from a battery into alternating current from the mains, thus making it possible to operate in the middle of nowhere or to keep on emitting even when the mains had been switched off.

The weak emitting power of the transmitter limited the range of the dangerous line-of-sight, direct wave. The great accuracy of the emitting frequency made it easier for the UK-based Home Station to locate and establish contact with the operators, even with a weak signal.

Below.
A Mk II set used from march to August 1943 in the Chambaran region of the Isère département.
(Laurent Rey, Musée de la Résistance de l'Isère collection)

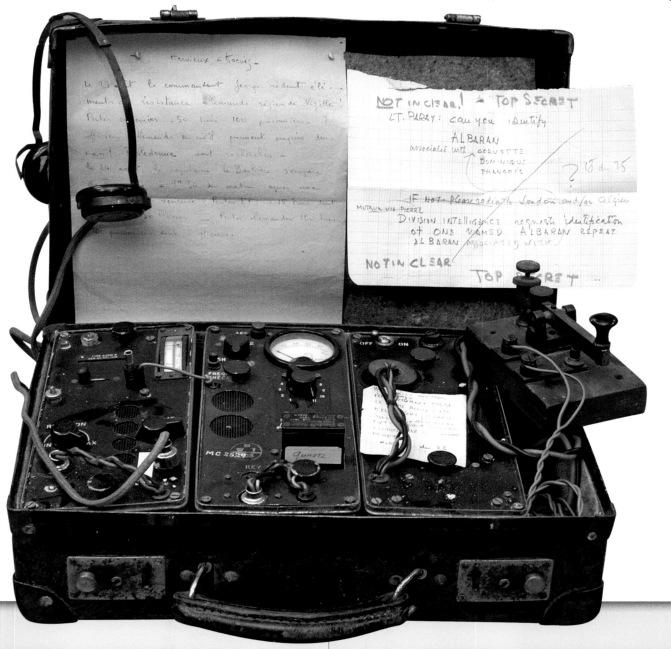

Country: Poland exiled in the United Kingdom
Type: AP 4 and AP 5
Organisation: Polish resistance, SOE, French, Czech, Italian, Albanian and Yugoslav resistance movements
Manufacturer: Polish Military Wireless Research Unit, Stanmore, England. (Polski Wojskowy Waarsztat Radiowy)
Designer: Tadeusz Heftman
Introduction: 1943
Power output: 8 - 12 W maximum
Emission frequency band: from 2 to 8 Mhz with 2 bands: 2 – 5 Mhz, 5 – 8 Mhz
Height: 9 cm
Length: 23 cm
Width: 10 cm
Weight: 1,6 kg

In 1943, the Stanmore Polish radio station produced 538 sets (of the A1, A2, A3 and AP 4 Type), mostly for the SOE.

Left.
Polish AP 4.
(Georges Ducrezet collection)

Next page.
Polish AP 5.
(Eric Pierret collection)

Country: Pologne exiled in the United Kingdom
Type: BP 3 and BP 4
Organisation: Polish resistance, SOE, French, Czech and Yugoslav resistance movements
Manufacturer: Polish Military Wireless Research Unit, Stanmore, England. (Polski Wojskowy Waarsztat Radiowy)
Designer: Tadeusz Heftman
Introduction: 1943
Power output:
50 W maximum
Power output:
from 2 to 8 Mhz with 2 bands: 2 – 5 Mhz, 5 – 8 Mhz
Height: 9,5 cm
Length: 21 cm
Width: 28 cm
Weight: 4 kg

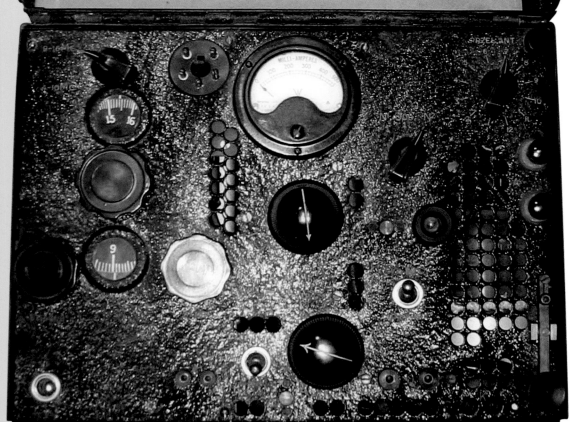

Left.
Polish BP 4.
(J-L. Perquin)

Country: United Kingdom
Type: Mk XV and Mk XVI
Organisation: MI6 SIS
Manufacturer: SIS Section VIII, Whaddon Hall/Little Horwood
Introduction: 1943
Power output: 15 W
Frequency band: 3,5 – 5,2 Mhz, 5 – 8 Mhz, 8 – 16 Mhz

The Mk XV existed in several versions; in a varnished plywood box, in an open-top steel box, in a steel box closed by a plywood lid or in an all-steel box. The final version (MK 16) was identical to the MK XV.

Receiver	**Transmitter**	**Adapter mains**
height: 12 cm	height: 13 cm	height: 14 cm
length: 14 cm	length: 16 cm	length: 16 cm
width: 22 cm	width: 29 cm	width: 30 cm
weight: 3,1 kg	weight: 3,4 kg	weight: 6,8 kg

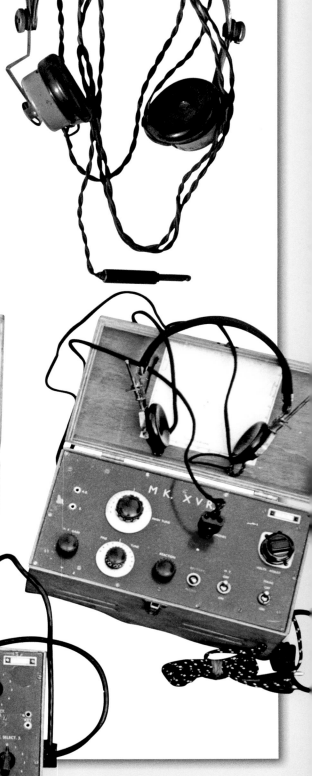

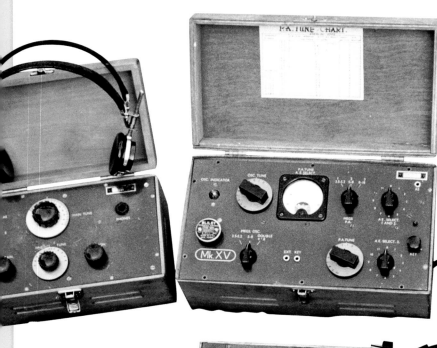

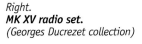

Right.
MK XV radio set.
(Georges Ducrezet collection)

Country: United Kingdom
Type: miniature receiver, Type M. C. R. 1 also known as "Receiver biscuit" or "Midget"
Organisation: SOE

This receiver owes its name to the fact it was delivered in 1 kg tin boxes of "Huntley-Palmers" biscuits that held:
- the receiver;
- four interchangeables bands;
- a headset;
- three batteries or two batteries and an adaptor for the main (97 to 250 volts alternating or continuous);
- a 9 metres flexible antenna wrapped round a Bakelite card; it had to be stretched on a length of at least two metres; if possible, the whole antenna was to be stretched;
- three meters of grounding cable which, when it was used, improved the quality of both reception and transmission.
Self 1 went from 150 KHz to 1,6 MHz (equivalent

Designer: Major John I. Brown, station IX, The Frythe, Welwyn
Manufacturer: Philco UK
Introduction: 1943

to long wave and medium wave of household radio sets).
Self 2 went from 2,5 to 4,5 MHz
Self 3 went from 4,5 to 8 MHz.
Self 4 went from 8 to 15 MHz.
The set was operated through four knobs; they controlled antenna adaptation, sensitivity, Morse code reception reaction and frequency. One 1-kg battery allowed for 30 hours in the "receive" mode.
- a 9 metres flexible antenna wrapped round a Bakelite card was also provided. It had to be stretched on a length of at least two metres; if possible, the whole antenna was to be stretched. The grounding cable was not mandatory but when it was used the quality of the reception and transmission improved.
Dimensions: 85 x 54 x 224 mm

Next page, top.
MCR1 "Biscuit" receiver. Notice the main adaptor, the 4 quartz, the receiver, the wire antenna, the headset and the famous biscuit tin.
(Museeradiomili collection)

Next page, top left.
Close up on the MCR 1 "Biscuit" set dry battery.
(J-L. Perquin, Patrick Lemaitre collection)

Receiver with self 1
height: 5 cm
length: 24 cm
width: 8 cm
weight: 0,9 kg

Adapter ACDC 38/1
height: 5 cm
length: 22 cm
width: 9 cm
weight: 1,7 kg

Dry cell battery
height: 5 cm
length: 19 cm
width: 5 cm
weight: 1 kg

Antenna length: 10 m.

Right.
A SAS Trooper takes note of a BBC "Broadcast" message received on a MCR1 "Biscuit" set connected to a B Type dry cell. A folding stock US M1-A1 Carbine rests on the jump helmet and the M-1911A1 .45 ACP pistol, US M3 combat knife and compass all remain close at hand ...
(Les Parachutistes SAS de la France libre, David Portier, Nimrod editions)

BATTERY, DRY
HT./LT. 90v/7½v
TYPE No. E.R.W. I520

Date of Manufacture

20 - 4 4

TYPE B.

Country: USA
Type: American RBZ receiver. Radio Receiving Equipment Frequency Range
Organisation: SOE
Manufacturer: Emerson Radio, NY, USA
Introduction: most probably 1943
Power output: 2 X 1.5 V batteries and 1 X 67.5 V battery
Frequency band: 5 – 13 MHz ou 3 – 6 MHz
Mode: AM/CW

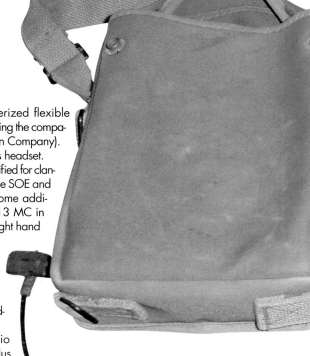

Waterproof radio receiver produced by the "Emerson Radio & Phonograph Corp." of New York City under US Navy contract Nxsx-15891. It had initially been designed for the Command and Control of amphibious units. These sets were meant to receive orders from the command ships during the early stages of beach assaults.

The set was made up of the following components:
- an "Olive Drab" waterproof carrying bag (CVH-10203)
- two interchangeable waterproof green plastic boxes containing:
- a CEX-46203 receiver with its on/off/volume and its frequency change knobs, its power supply cable and the antenna plug.
- a CEX-10172 power supply with two A Type 1.5 Volt round batteries and one Type B 67.5 Volts flat square battery, a headset cord and a second plug for the connection with the emitter.

- a CEX-49238 rubberized flexible antenna cable, (CEX being the company code of the Emerson Company).
- a CVH-10204 canvas headset.

This set was then modified for clandestine operations by the SOE and the OSS. It received some additional markings: 5 – 13 MC in orange colour on the right hand side of the dial (modification of the frequency band from 3 – 6 MHz to 5 – 13 MHz which made it possible to receive the BBC's "Broadcast" messages).

In 1947 those radio sets were sold as surplus for the sum of 11.95 $ apiece, without batteries.

Below.
Close up on the orange 5-13 MC markings on the right hand side of the dial of Francois Chatelin's radio set. This marking meant that the frequencies had been modified for SOE/OSS clandestine use.
(J.-L. Perquin)

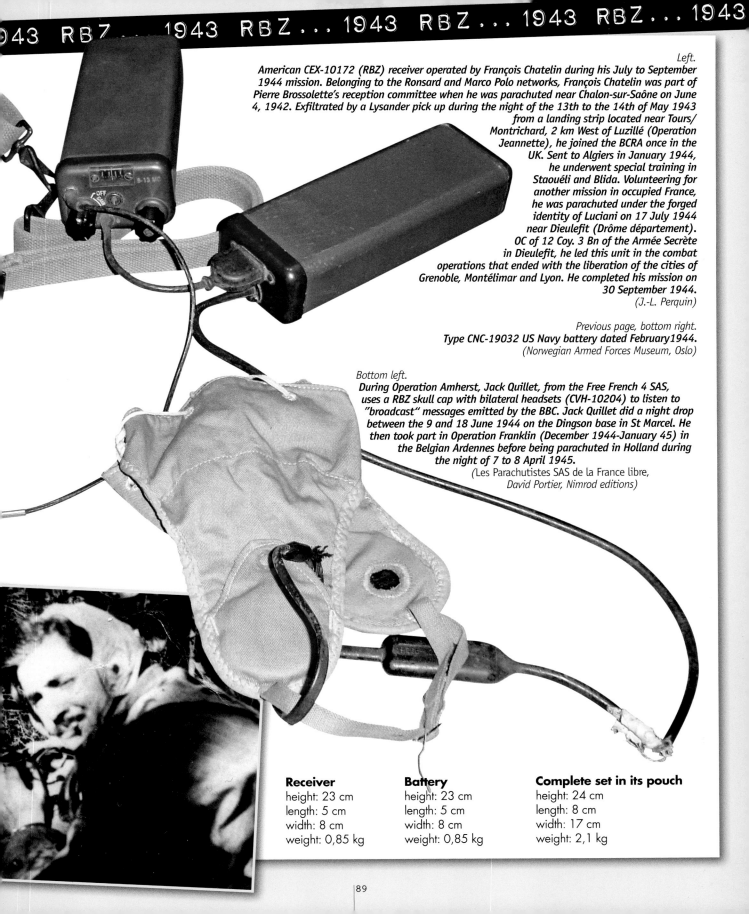

Left.
American CEX-10172 (RBZ) receiver operated by François Chatelin during his July to September 1944 mission. Belonging to the Ronsard and Marco Polo networks, François Chatelin was part of Pierre Brossolette's reception committee when he was parachuted near Chalon-sur-Saône on June 4, 1942. Exfiltrated by a Lysander pick up during the night of the 13th to the 14th of May 1943 from a landing strip located near Tours/ Montrichard, 2 km West of Luzillé (Operation Jeannette), he joined the BCRA once in the UK. Sent to Algiers in January 1944, he underwent special training in Staouéli and Blida. Volunteering for another mission in occupied France, he was parachuted under the forged identity of Luciani on 17 July 1944 near Dieulefit (Drôme département). OC of 12 Coy. 3 Bn of the Armée Secrète in Dieulefit, he led this unit in the combat operations that ended with the liberation of the cities of Grenoble, Montélimar and Lyon. He completed his mission on 30 September 1944.
(J.-L. Perquin)

Previous page, bottom right.
Type CNC-19032 US Navy battery dated February1944.
(Norwegian Armed Forces Museum, Oslo)

Bottom left.
During Operation Amherst, Jack Quillet, from the Free French 4 SAS, uses a RBZ skull cap with bilateral headsets (CVH-10204) to listen to "broadcast" messages emitted by the BBC. Jack Quillet did a night drop between the 9 and 18 June 1944 on the Dingson base in St Marcel. He then took part in Operation Franklin (December 1944-January 45) in the Belgian Ardennes before being parachuted in Holland during the night of 7 to 8 April 1945.
(Les Parachutistes SAS de la France libre, David Portier, Nimrod editions)

Receiver
height: 23 cm
length: 5 cm
width: 8 cm
weight: 0,85 kg

Battery
height: 23 cm
length: 5 cm
width: 8 cm
weight: 0,85 kg

Complete set in its pouch
height: 24 cm
length: 8 cm
width: 17 cm
weight: 2,1 kg

Country: United Kingdom, Norway
Type: type 31/1 receiver "Sweetheart"
Organisation: SOE
Designer: Norwegian engineer Willy Simonsen
Manufacturer: Hale Electric Co Ltd
Introduction: 1943
Antenna lenght: 10 m

The headset is of a standard type produced by the Brush Company in the USA. It was held in a sealed tobacco tin and the orders were never to open this tin when the altitude was higher than 2,500 metres. The receiver had no on/off button but it was disconnected when the power supply was unplugged. The batteries were standard to occupied areas household torch light batteries with a life expectancy of about 50 hours.

Receiver	Battery	Complete set
height: 3 cm	height: 2,5 cm	height: 8 cm
length: 14 cm	length: 10 cm	length: 19 cm
width: 11 cm	width: 8 cm	width: 14 cm
width: 0,5 kg	width: 0,4 kg	width: 41,8 kg

Below.
Ever Ready brand batteries dated June 5, 1944 for an RCD 31/1 "Sweetheart" receiver.
(Norwegian Armed Forces Museum Oslo)

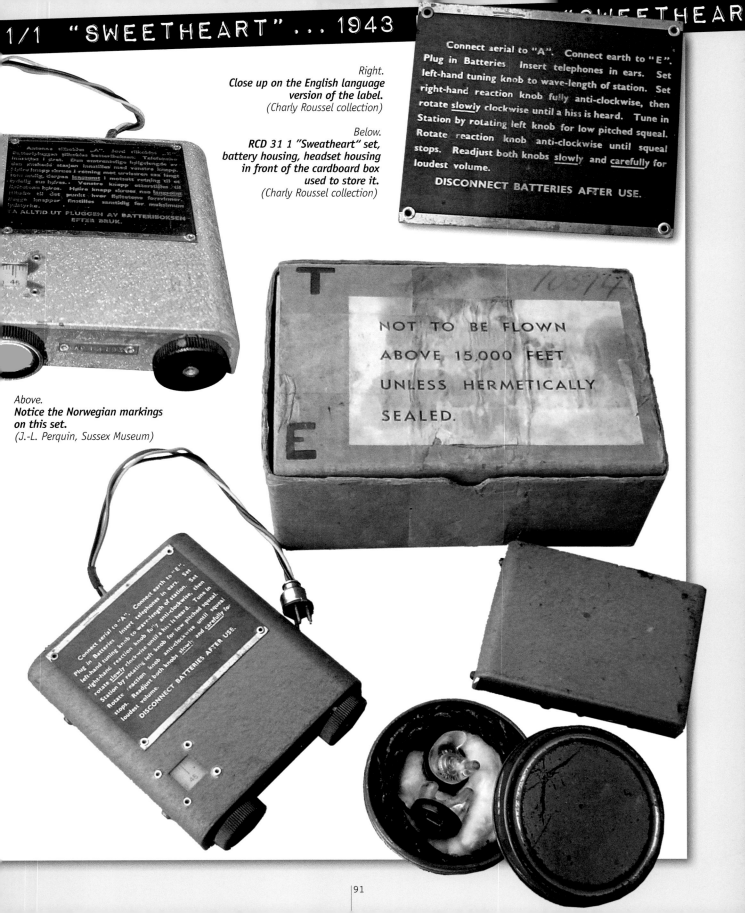

Right.
Close up on the English language version of the label.
(Charly Roussel collection)

Below.
RCD 31 1 "Sweatheart" set, battery housing, headset housing in front of the cardboard box used to store it.
(Charly Roussel collection)

Connect aerial to "A". Connect earth to "E". Plug in Batteries. Insert telephones in ears. Set left-hand tuning knob to wave-length of station. Set right-hand reaction knob fully anti-clockwise, then rotate <u>slowly</u> clockwise until a hiss is heard. Tune in Station by rotating left knob for low pitched squeal. Rotate reaction knob anti-clockwise until squeal stops. Readjust both knobs <u>slowly</u> and <u>carefully</u> for loudest volume.

DISCONNECT BATTERIES AFTER USE.

Above.
Notice the Norwegian markings on this set.
(J.-L. Perquin, Sussex Museum)

NOT TO BE FLOWN
ABOVE 15,000 FEET
UNLESS HERMETICALLY
SEALED.

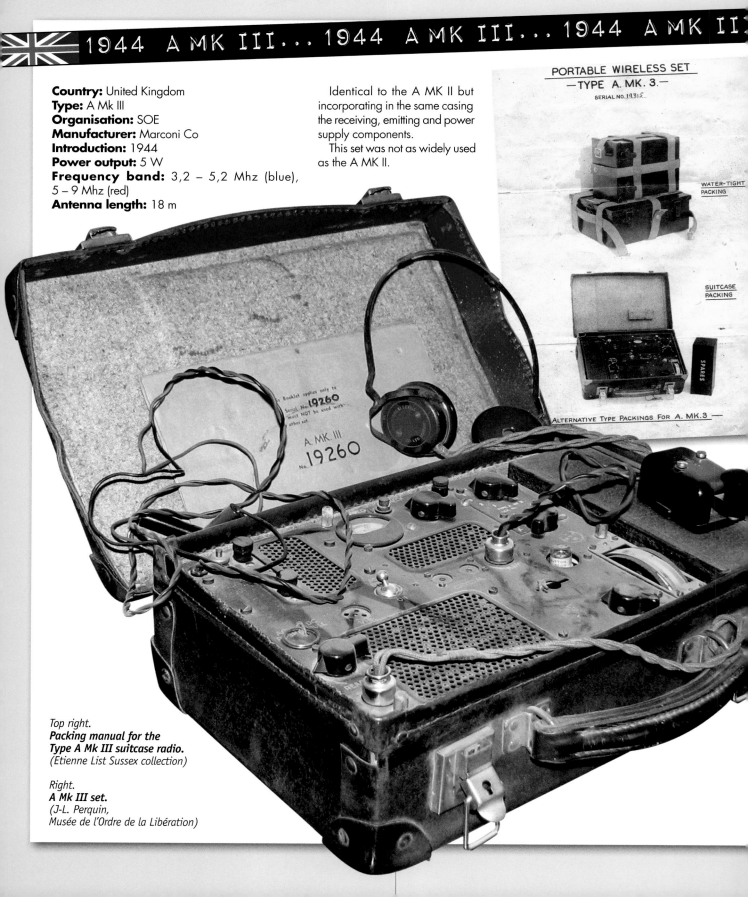

Country: United Kingdom
Type: A Mk III
Organisation: SOE
Manufacturer: Marconi Co
Introduction: 1944
Power output: 5 W
Frequency band: 3,2 – 5,2 Mhz (blue), 5 – 9 Mhz (red)
Antenna length: 18 m

Identical to the A MK II but incorporating in the same casing the receiving, emitting and power supply components.

This set was not as widely used as the A MK II.

PORTABLE WIRELESS SET
—TYPE A. MK. 3.—
SERIAL No. 19315.

WATER-TIGHT PACKING

SUITCASE PACKING

SPARES

ALTERNATIVE TYPE PACKINGS FOR A. MK.3.—

Top right.
Packing manual for the Type A Mk III suitcase radio.
(Etienne List Sussex collection)

Right.
A Mk III set.
(J-L. Perquin, Musée de l'Ordre de la Libération)

Transmitter-Receiver
height: 9 cm
length: 19,5 cm
width: 23 cm
weight: 3,8 kg

Power source
height: 9 cm
length: 18 cm
width: 7 cm
weight: 1 kg

Complete suitcase
height: 11 cm
length: 24 cm
width: 33 cm
weight: 6,5 kg

**Set in a "C"
Type container**
height: 11,5 cm
length: 24 cm
width: 29 cm
weight: 6,5 kg

**Accessories in a "D"
Type container**
height: 23 cm
length: 14,5 cm
width: 18 cm
weight: 5,1 kg

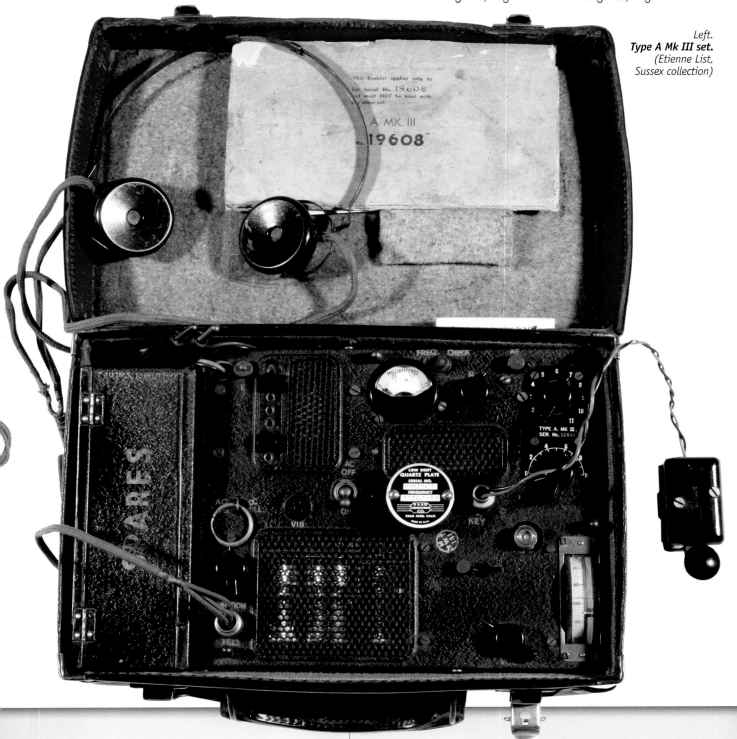

Left.
Type A Mk III set.
*(Etienne List,
Sussex collection)*

Left.
A Mk III set in its "Para" version which was held in two metal boxes; box C for the transmitter and receiver and box D for the accessories.
(Museeradiomili collection)

Below.
Type A Mk III suitcase radio operator manual and tips to improve the quality of the emission.
(Etienne List, Sussex collection)

Below.
Type A Mk III suitcase radio original manual
(Etienne List, Sussex collection)

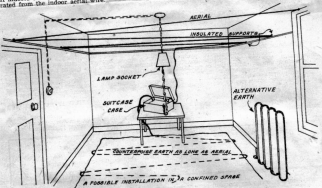

THE EARTH.
An efficient earth is most important. The ideal would be to solder a short length of wire to a large sheet of copper buried in moist earth near to the transmitter and to attach the free end of the wire to the earth terminal of the transmitter. Failing this, a copper earth tube, a large coil of barbed wire, an old oil drum well scraped, or some such metal receptical could be buried instead, but it is most important that where it is attached to the earthwire should be clean metal, a good electrical contact, preferably soldered should be made and that the ground should be moist.

If indoors, a water pipe may be convenient. Choose a cold water pipe near to the ground if possible, rather than a hot pipe which may be loosely attached to dry walls in several places before finally making a good earth connection. Scrape the pipe clean before attaching the earth wire.

If no pipes are available a length of wire arrayed in zig-zag fashion or a piece of wire netting may be placed underneath the floor covering and attached to the transmitter by a short earth wire. An efficient counterpoise earth may be made by arranging a wire of about the same length as the aerial wire, and insulated from earthed objects underneath the aerial wire and 2 or 3 feet above the ground. If indoors the counterpoise earth should be on the floor—perhaps under the carpet and well separated from the indoor aerial wire.

AERIAL
INSULATED SUPPORTS
LAMP SOCKET
ALTERNATIVE EARTH
SUITCASE CASE
COUNTERPOISE EARTH AS LONG AS AERIAL
A POSSIBLE INSTALLATION IN A CONFINED SPACE

This Booklet applies only to
Set Serial No. **19315**
and must NOT be used with any other set.

A. MK. III
No. **19315**

Country: United Kingdom
Type: PCR
Organisation: British Army and Résistance movements
Manufacturer: Pye ltd et Philips Lamps ltd
Introduction: 1944
Frequency band: 850 metres to 5,8 Mhz
Antenna length: 10 – 30 m

This set was designed for the armed forces to be able to receive Broadcast messages. A small number was dropped to Résistance movements in France, Norway and Holland in order to listen to BBC messages. The set is packed in a flat black painted metal box.

Receiver	**Voltage transformer**	**Adapter**
height: 21 cm	height: 21 cm	height: 21 cm
length: 32 cm	length: 32 cm	length: 32 cm
width: 44 cm	width: 44 cm	width: 15 cm
weight: 11,4 kg	weight: 10,4 kg	weight: 8 kg

Below.
***British PCR set
found in the Ardèche
departement of France.***
*(Pascal Drouvain picture
and collection)*

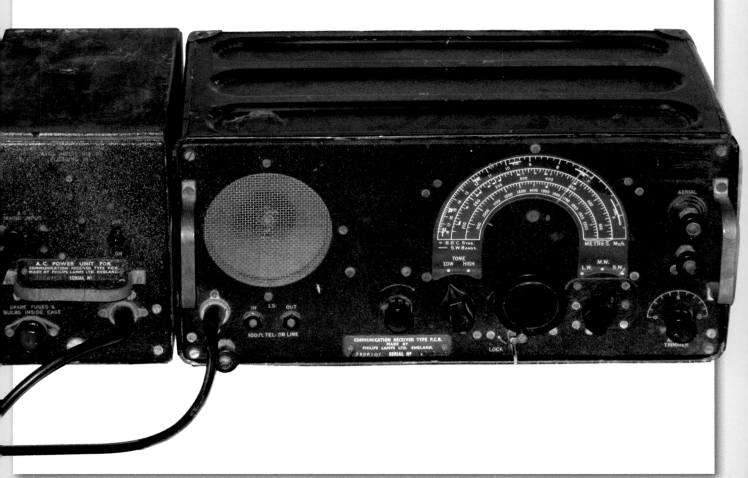

Country: USA
Type: AN/PRC-5
Organisation: American Intelligence Agencies-
Manufacturer: Circa
Introduction: 1944
Power output: 16 W (10 W for D and D')
Reception frequency band: 4,5 – 16 Mhz

Emission frequency band: 4 – 16 Mhz
B: 4 – 6 Mhz   D: 8 – 12 Mhz
C: 6 – 8 Mhz   D': 12 – 16 Mhz
Antenna lenght: 50 m
Height: 10,5 cm
Length: 27,9 cm
Width: 25,4 cm
Weight: 11,3 kg

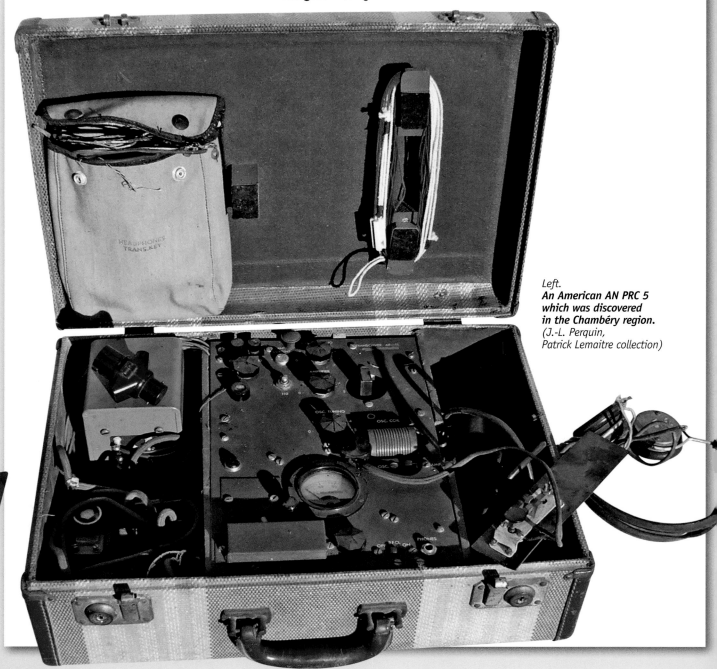

Left.
An American AN PRC 5
which was discovered
in the Chambéry region.
(J.-L. Perquin,
Patrick Lemaitre collection)

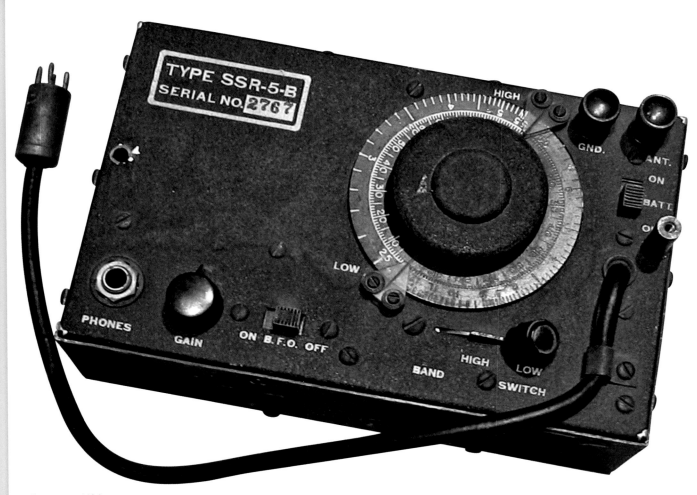

Country: USA
Type: SSTR-5
Organisation: OSS
Manufacturer: Circa
Introduction: 1944
Power output: roughly 0,5 W
Frequency band: 2,5 – 12 Mhz
Antenna lenght: 17 m

The smallest radio set ever designed by the OSS. Very few information are available on its actual operational use.

Above.
SSR 5 B Receiver of the American SSTR-5 set.
(J.-L. Perquin)

SST-5 Transmitter
height: 8,9 cm
length: 19,1 cm
width: 11,7 cm
weight: 1,25 kg

SST-5 Receiver
height: 8,9 cm
length: 19,1 cm
width: 11,7 cm
weight: 1,25 kg

Country: United Kingdom
Organisation: SOE
Type: 46/1 "Jedburgh" and 48/1 "Nicholls"
Manufacturer: SOE Stonebridge Park (except for the MCR1)
Introduction: 1944
Power output: 8-10 W for the 46/1 "Jed Set" and 11 W for the 48/1 "Nicholls"
Frequency band:
- 46/1 "Jed Set"   48/1 "Nicholls"
- 3 – 5 Mhz, 3 – 16 Mhz
- 5 – 9 Mhz
Weight: 16,8 kg for the 46/1 et 20,2 Kg for the 48/1
Antenna length: 25 m

Designs to be issued to Jedburgh teams, the two sets were almost identical, the main differences being found in the transmitter. The emitter was a MCR1 Biscuit set and the various components were held in five Web canvas pouches that could be adapted to the standard British Army load carrying equipment so that one man could carry the complete set. If necessary, the various components could also be shared among a team. Designed with the freedom of movement of the teams in mind, the set was provided with a hand-cranked generator for the transmitter as well as dry cell batteries for the MCR1.

1st pouch: MCR1 with two dry cell batteries and accessories
2nd pouch: 46/1 or 48/1 transmitter and 25 m of wire antenna
3rd pouch: "Hand Generator 45/III"
4th pouch: Telescopic tripod for the hand-cranked generator
5th pouch: Two-part telescopic antenna.

Below.
MCR1 with its Web pouch. This is the receiver part of the "Jed set". Notice the metal box containing spare parts including a headset as well as the American CVH-10204 headset, which was normally associated with the RBZ set.
(Bertrand Souquet collection)

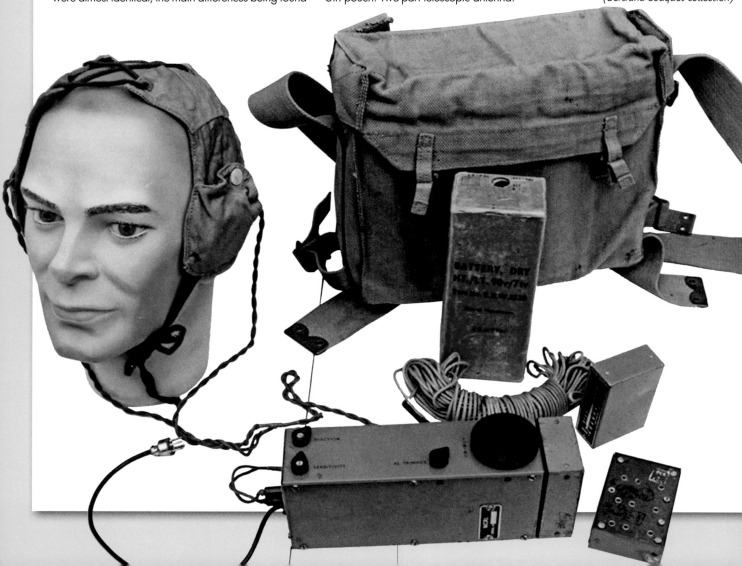

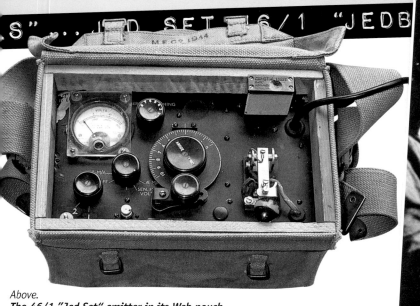

Above.
The 46/1 "Jed Set" emitter in its Web pouch.
(J-L. Perquin, Georges Ducrezet collection)

Right.
During Operation Moses, SAS Trooper Maurice Obadia from 3 SAS operates a Jed set. Parachuted during the night of 2 to 3 August 1944 near a Maquis North of Asnieres-sur-Blour, Maurice Obadia was to be severely wounded by four bullets as well as several grenade fragments while attacking a German position in Coussay les Bois on September 4, 1944.
(Book "Les Parachutistes SAS de la France Libre", David Portier, Nimrod edition)

Above.
46/1 "Jed set" 46/1 emitter and 45/III hand cranked generator on its tripod.
(J-L. Perquin, Georges Ducrezet collection)

Right.
MCR1 receiver of a Jed set in its Web pouch. This particular set was operated by Second Lieutenant Jacques Morineau "Luc", a radio operator of the Cinnamon mission. He was parachuted on 13 August 1944 with British Captain Robert Harcourt "Louis" and French Captain Lespinasse Fonsegrive "Orthon" on DZ "Fantôme" in Brue Auriac, 10 km from St Maximin (Var département). Harcourt broke both his legs on landing...
(Bertrand Souquet collection)

Left.
45/III hand cranked generator on its tripod.
(J-L. Perquin, Georges Ducrezet collection)

Right.
**The 5 pouches that made up
the Jed set could be fitted
to a single man.**
(Jean Sassi collection)

Previous page, top.
**During Operation Amherst, after having been
parachuted during the night of 7 to 8 April 1945
near Assen, Holland, the "Archivist 36" radio team
belonging to the Free French 2nd RCP/4 SAS is seen
here operating a Jed-set. From left to right: Charles
Collignon operating a 46/1 transmitter, Jo Lalisse
holding the characteristic tripod-mounted hand cranked
electric generator "Hand Generator 45/III" and André
Renaud, the station chief, wearing a RBZ canvas
headset (CVH-10204) connected to a British MCR1
receiver nicknamed the "Biscuit".The association of the
RBZ skull cap with bilateral headsets with the MCR1
seems to have been a common practice with Jed-Set
since out of four known pictures of those equipments
being used, three illustrate that combination!**
*(Book "Les Parachutistes SAS de la France Libre",
David Portier, Nimrod editions)*

Country: United Kingdom
Manufacturer: Masteradio
Year of production: 1940

Reception Set R103 was a small HF receiver designed for monitoring applications in British Army non-combat vehicles such as staff cars. The equipment covers the frequency range 1.7 - 7.5MHz in two switched ranges. It used an external power supply, which operated from a 12 Volt DC supply. It also contained a loudspeaker. This set was used to listen to BBC OC emissions as well as night telegraphic broadcasts since it was fitted with a BFO. This set had two different designation within the BCRA since it was distributed in two versions including a covert one which was meant to look like a commercial radio. One set was known as the VOX (R103 A receiver, covert version) and the VOXNU (R103 MARK II receiver with 12 V battery).

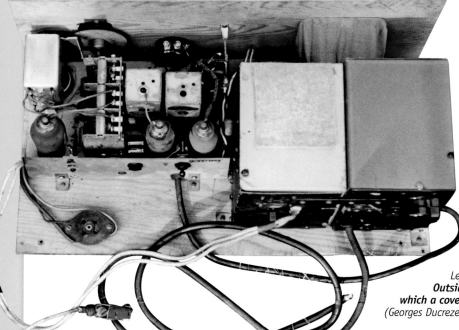

Left.
Outside view of an inocuous-looking radio set inside which a covert radio set has been hidden.
(Georges Ducrezet collection)

Inventory of the radio sets and associated equipment supplied by RF Section between October 1943 and September 1944

386	A Mk II	248	hand cranked generators
212	A Mk III	48	steam generators
87	A Mk I Star	839	battery chargers
188	B Mk II	1947	batteries
124	R 103	2768	MCR 1
87	petrol generators	114	S-Phones
92	pedal generators	77	Eureka

Above.
Type A Mk III radio set ready to operate.
(Georges Ducrezet picture and collection)

Some remarks as a preamble ; first of all, a little known radio set appears, the R 103 ; a microfilm reveals that this set existed in two versions, either camouflaged or not. The absence of RBZ RCD 31/1 "Sweetheart" receivers is also noteworthy as they can be found in numbers on the field ; the same comment is also true for the Emerson 455 and the RCA BP-10 Victor.

For example, Rivière, alias Marquis, used at least two such sets, one being now in the care of the *Musée de l'Ordre de la Libération* in Paris and the other being held in storage by the *Centre d'Histoire de la Résistance et de la Déportation* in Lyons. Finally, this list deals solely with the radio sets and associated equipment supplied by the RF Section (BCRA) and one could be forgiven for thinking that at least an equal quantity of equipment was sent to Section F, better known as the "Buckmaster networks". The S-Phone and the Eureka are ground-to-air radio sets and they will be dealt with in the next book of this series which will deal with parachute drops and covert landing operations.

Right.
Receiver hidden inside a commercial looking radio set.
(François Dujardin picture and collection)

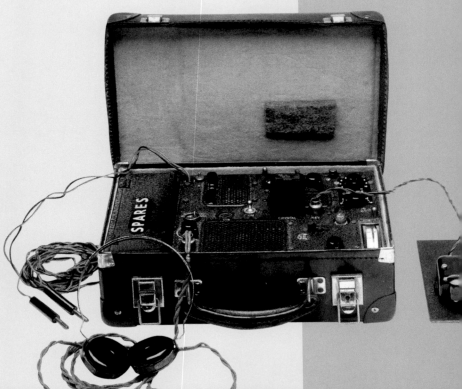

Left.
HST 40 6V 5A Hand cranked generator in use in a Greek resistance movement.
(IWM HU-67330)

Left.
Carrying pouch for a hand cranked generator.
(Vinje Museum, Norway)

Bottom left.
Operating manual of a hand cranked generator.
(Vinje Museum, Norway)

Opposite page, top left and center.
Close up on a generator with bicycle adapter.
(Musée de la Résistance et de la Déportation de l'Ain collection)

Opposite page, top right.
July 1944, a B2 set battery is being charged. Maurice Mercier "Peruvien" is on the bicycle; André Lacour is top left, Jean Cendral, "Lombard", who was parachuted on 5 May 1944 on "Temple" near Allex, in the Drôme département, is at the bottom; Mario Montefusco "Argentin" or Titin, who was parachuted on 11 November 1943 in the Pavin Lake area in the Puy de Dôme département and who was the head of the "BCRA Londres" signal network in the Vercors, is visible on the right.
(Pierre Lassale)

Opposite page, bottom right.
The generator with a bicycle adapter ready for use.
(IWM)

Opposite page, bottom left.
HST 40 6V 5A Hand cranked generator. It had a power output of 6 Volts at 5 Amperes.
(Vinje Museum, Norway)

There were several types of hand-cranked generators: the Battery Charger N°1, the Hand Generator Type 37/1 and the Generator 20 watts, Type C Mk I. Their weight was comprised between 2,5 and 5 kg. At 80 rpm, they could charge a 6 volts battery at 2,5 to 3 amperes. Two types of generators used a pedal system. One had to be adapted on to a normal bicycle; the other was a stand alone system complete with a tripod and a bicycle seat.

Left.
This C MK I MOL hand cranked generator was dropped on the "Faisan" DZ in the Marne département.
(Musée de l'Ordre de la Libération collection)

HAND GENERATOR
(Hoover Battery Charger No. 2)

SPECIFICATION.

This equipment, for charging a 6-volt battery, consists of a small generator with a totally enclosed 40 to 1 step-up gear box, to which can be fastened a handle and two table clamps. The whole, together with battery leads and spare carbon brushes, is packed into a felt lined steel watertight container.

INSTALLATION.

1. Open the container and withdraw the clamps, handle, generator, leads and small linen bag.

2. From the bag take the 4 bolts and 4 distance pieces.

3. With the front bracket of the generator flat on a bench or table, attach the clamps vertically to the gear box end with the distance pieces between the brackets and the gear box, so that the clamping screws can be adjusted to grip the underside of the table.

4. Fix the handle, ensuring that the keyway is engaged and the bolt tightened. Note: This bolt has a left-hand thread, hence it is necessary to screw it in a counter-clockwise direction.

5. Attach the ring tag on the red (+ve) lead to the generator terminal marked L+ and the black (−ve) lead to the terminal marked A−.

OUTPUT.

7 volts 3 amps. approx. at 100 r.p.m. of the handle.

OPERATING INSTRUCTIONS : Charging a 6-volt battery.

1. Check the acid level in the battery, and if it is low, due to evaporation, add distilled water, or clean rain water.

2. Clean the battery terminals and attach the Red (+ve) clip to the +ve terminal of the battery and the other (−ve) clip to the −ve terminal.

3. At once begin turning the handle in a clockwise direction.

NOTE : Unless the battery is fully discharged when the second clip is attached the battery will drive the generator and the handle will turn. This is discharging the battery still further and either it should be disconnected at once or the handle turned more rapidly.

MAINTENANCE.

The generator should require little or no maintenance other than an occasional cleaning of the commutator. To do this:

1. Remove the two brass commutator cover plates from the end of the generator remote from the handle.

2. Take out the bolts holding the brush leads.

3. Raise and move sideways the brush retaining springs.

4. Withdraw the carbon brushes.

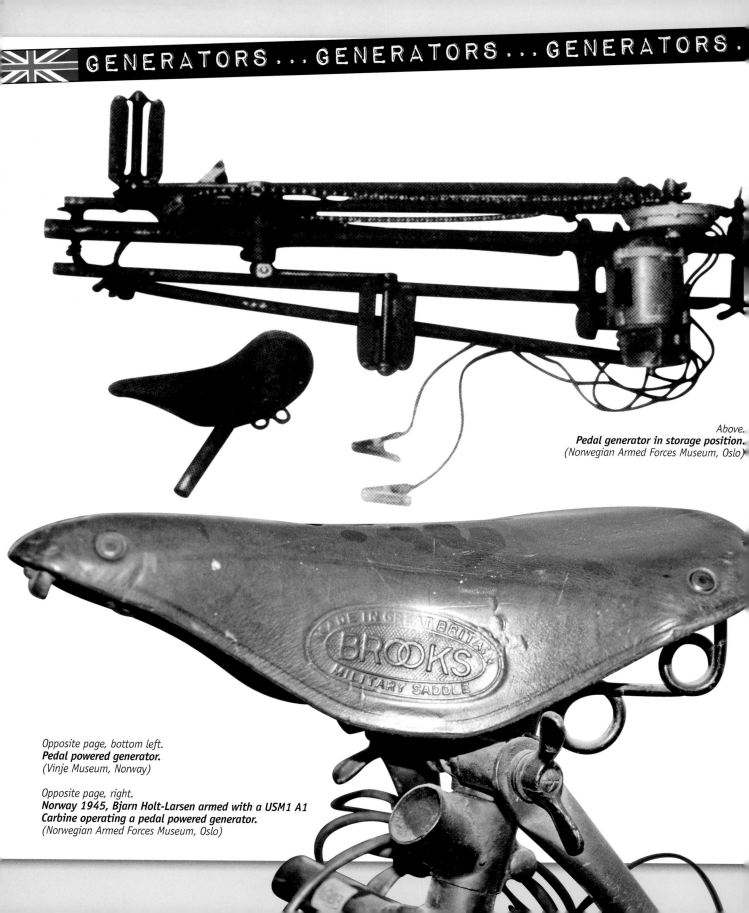

Above.
Pedal generator in storage position.
(Norwegian Armed Forces Museum, Oslo)

Opposite page, bottom left.
Pedal powered generator.
(Vinje Museum, Norway)

Opposite page, right.
**Norway 1945, Bjarn Holt-Larsen armed with a USM1 A1
Carbine operating a pedal powered generator.**
(Norwegian Armed Forces Museum, Oslo)

BATTERY CHARGER № 1

OUTPUT 7V. 3A.

AT 1950 R.P.M.

SERIAL № L.H. 2828

Country: United Kingdom
Type: ALCO Steam Generator
Organisation: SOE
Manufacturer: Arthur Lyon & Co, Londres
Introduction: 1944

This generator was capable of charging 6 volts batteries using nothing but wood and water. Considering the water tank could only hold 13, 5 litres of water and that the generator needed 4,5 litres of water per hour, it was thus necessary to stop the generator every 2,5 hours to refill it with water.

Below.
ALCO Steam Generator.
(Stein Aasland, Norges Hjemmefrontmuseum)

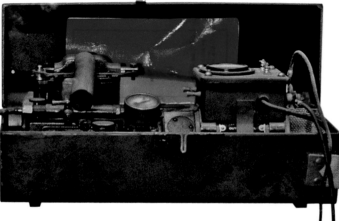

Below.
ALCO Steam Generator in front of a bicycle fitted with a generator adapter.
(Musée de la Résistance et de la Déportation de Nantua)

Water tank
height: 41 cm
length: 25 cm
width: 15,9 cm

Frame
height: 46 cm
length: 36 cm
width: 11,4 cm

Complete set
height: 46 cm
length: 36 cm
width: 40,8 cm

Generator
height: 18 cm
length: 38 cm
width: 14 cm
weight: 13,5 kg

Power Generator
Dimensions: 71 x 38 cm
Weight: 37 kg
Power output: with a consumption of 2 to 3 pints of petrol an hour, it could charge a 12 Volt battery to 6/7 Ampere.

Above.
On this picture taken in the Aisne Maquis, it is possible to identify a RB 8 Petrol Generator in the foreground as well as a "Heayberd" rectifier on the table.
(George Ricard)

Right.
Produced by F.C Heayberd and Co. London. It converted alternating 110/220 Volts 50 Hz current to direct 2,6 and 12 Volts current.
(Stein Aasland, Norwegian Armed Forces Museum, Oslo)